Annie Howells and Achille Fréchette

Annie Howells and Achille Fréchette

JAMES DOYLE

University of Toronto Press
Toronto Buffalo London

© University of Toronto Press 1979
Toronto Buffalo London
Printed in Canada

Canadian Cataloguing in Publication Data

Doyle, James, 1937–
Annie Howells and Achille Fréchette

Bibliography: p.
Includes index.
ISBN 0-8020-5450-1
1. Fréchette, Annie Howells.
2. Fréchette, Achille.
I. Title.
FC3096.41.F74D69   971.3'84'050924   C79-094238-0
F1059.5.09D69

To Margaret

Contents

Preface

In June 1877, at the American consulate in Quebec City, Annie Thomas Howells of Jefferson, Ohio, married Achille Fréchette of Ottawa, Ontario. The bride was the daughter of the American consul in Quebec William Cooper Howells, and the sister of the rising young American novelist William Dean Howells; the groom, originally from Lévis, and in 1877 an employee in the translation department of the Canadian House of Commons, was the brother of the acclaimed French-Canadian poet Louis Fréchette. Both Annie Howells and Achille Fréchette were authors in their own right: the new bride had written and published a novel in 1876 while living at the consulate and was a regular contributor of short stories and feature articles to various magazines and newspapers in the United States; her husband had been a French-language journalist in Chicago and Ottawa before entering the Canadian civil service and had published poems in various Canadian periodicals. In keeping with the strong traditions of literary activity in their respective families, and with their own artistic inclinations, both husband and wife continued to pursue part-time writing careers throughout their lives, and Achille achieved minor recognition as a portrait painter.

The interest of the Fréchettes to posterity, however, does not lie chiefly in their respective achievements in literature and art – although those achievements were by no means negligible – but in their intensive involvement in the cultural life of both Canada and the United States in the late nineteenth and early twentieth centuries. The lives and careers of these two individuals, spanning two countries and more than three-quarters of a century, serve as a concise synthesis of Canadian and American responses to an era of rapid industrial change, political expansion, and cultural development. The American Middle West into which Annie Howells was born is generally associated with the radical or 'Jacksonian' egalitarian democracy of the frontier and with a commitment to the myths and ideologies of progress. The tradition in which Achille Fréchette was nourished is identifiable with the development of Canadian Liberalism from the administration of Alexander Mackenzie through the age of Wilfrid Laurier, a development based on belief in material progress, advocacy of economic and cultural rapprochement with the United States, secularization of French-Canadian society and culture, and attempts at reconciliation of French- and English-Canadian differences. Yet, as intensive studies of these countries and periods reveal, none of these generalizations comes close to being conclusive: at best, they provide only one set of terms in a complex dialectic. Jacksonian democracy and the American frontier, besides being the breeding ground for aggressively liberal ideas, produced certain conservative intellectual traditions and social actions. In a comparable way, Canadian Liberalism was committed to the preservation of nationalistic traditions and values, such as loyalty to the British Empire, the survival of French-Canadian culture, and the development of a Canadian identity distinct from its American counterpart.

The complexity of this dialectic is also demonstrated by the literary relationships of Annie Howells and Achille Fréchette. From the perspective of the twentieth century, both William Dean Howells and Louis Fréchette are frequently associated with the notion of cultural establishments in their respective countries, and with a 'genteel' and therefore apparently devitalized kind of writing. It is thus easy to forget that both these writers were in their time controversial literary iconoclasts. Howells' brand of relentlessly documentary realism provoked shock and dismay among a generation of Americans nourished on the insipidities of sentimental romanticism, and he had to fight a continuous critical battle for at least twenty-five years to have his artistic theories and practices widely accepted. Similarly, the exuberant poetic nationalism of Louis Fréchette was sometimes associated, especially by ecclesiastical authorities in French Canada, with anticlericalism, republicanism, and other subversive tendencies. Annie Howells and Achille Fréchette, in their comparatively minor literary efforts, were inevitably influenced by the work of their respective brothers, while at the same time frequently deferential to other powerful cultural forces emanating especially from the influential magazines and newspapers of Canada and the United States. Accordingly, their writings often very concisely display prominent elements of the most important literary developments and controversies of the day. In addition, their correspondence with their two brothers (particularly the numerous surviving letters between Annie and William Dean Howells) often presents revealing observations on literary and other topics.

The lives and careers of Annie Howells and Achille Fréchette are also related to a fairly wide North American geographical arena, encompassing Chicago, Boston, Quebec City, and especially Ottawa, where they lived for almost forty years. In the late nineteenth and early twentieth centuries, the Canadian capital was a virtual paradigm of the nation as a whole, being an intriguing amalgamation of raw frontier town and expanding modern city, as well as the focus of important Canadian cultural and political aspirations. Many prominent people of interest to political as well as cultural history were in Ottawa during these years, and came within the Fréchettes' social circle. Their friends included, for instance, political figures like Wilfrid Laurier, scholars like John G. Bourinot, and poets such as Archibald Lampman and Duncan Campbell Scott.

But besides being representative of their place and time, and being involved with many important cultural and political figures, Annie Howells and Achille Fréchette were also interesting individuals, whose joint biography well deserves to be told for its own sake. Fortunately for the biographer and cultural historian, these two people were aware of the possible interest of their literary and personal relationships to posterity and anxious to preserve a detailed record of their lives and careers. They were also, in accordance with a widespread nineteenth-century fashion, inexhaustible writers of letters, and the immense quantity of their surviving correspondence provides a fascinating chronicle of their lives, their relationships, and their era, extending over a period of more than sixty years.

In the research, writing and publication of this work I have received assistance from a great many sources, for which it is now my pleasant duty to express my appreciation.

I am grateful to the Canada Council for a research and travel grant in the 1976–7 university year, and to Wilfrid Laurier University for two summer research fellowships, in 1976 and 1977.

The manuscript divisions of the following libraries allowed me the use of their facilities and access to their Howells-Fréchette material: the Huntington Library; the Houghton Library at Harvard; the Public Archives of Canada (with special thanks to Ms Anne Goddard); and the

Library of Congress, Washington, DC. The following libraries provided photocopies of the Howells-Fréchette papers in their possession: the New York Public Library; the Ohio Historical Society; the Rutherford B. Hayes Library, Fremont, Ohio. I must also gratefully acknowledge assistance from the staff of the newspapers division of the National Library of Canada.

It is my particular pleasure to express gratitude for the very kind assistance of Professor Van Derck Fréchette of Alfred University, Alfred, New York, who gave me unlimited access to the immense collection of his grandparents' papers in his possession. Quotations from the unpublished writings of Annie Howells and Achille Fréchette, as well as the photographs in this volume, are used with the generous permission of Professor Fréchette and Mr William Dean Howells Fréchette. Quotations from unpublished William Dean Howells manuscript material in the Houghton Library are used by permission of the Houghton Library; excerpts from unpublished Howells manuscripts located in other repositories are quoted with the permission of Professor William White Howells. Anyone seeking to quote from any of the sources mentioned above must obtain permission from the previously named authorities.

I am grateful to the editors of *Atlantis* for allowing me to reprint the part of chapter 4 which appeared as an article in that journal. I would like to extend my thanks to David McNab, who read portions of this work in manuscript and gave me the benefit of his knowledge of nineteenth-century Canadian political and social history. My wife, Margaret, besides contributing invaluable encouragement throughout the research and writing, read the entire manuscript and suggested numerous stylistic improvements.

This book has been published with the help of a grant from the Canadian Federation for the Humanities, using funds provided by the Social Sciences and Humanities Research Council of Canada, and a grant from the Andrew W. Mellon Foundation to the University of Toronto Press.

William Cooper Howells, about 1870

Annie Howells, about 1876

Achille Fréchette, about 1876

Edmond Fréchette, NWMP, 1881

TOP the Fréchette home
at 87 MacKay Street, Ottawa

BOTTOM Annie and Marie-Marguerite
at 87 MacKay Street, about 1891

Annie Howells Fréchette, 1894

Achille, Annie, and Marie-Marguerite
in the living room at 87 MacKay Street,
about 1896

Achille Fréchette:

ABOVE about 1910

TOP LEFT about 1900

LEFT in the study at 87 MacKay Street, about 1905

Annie Howells Fréchette:

ABOVE in Ottawa, 1913

TOP LEFT at Lausanne, Switzerland, 1912

LEFT with Achille in Switzerland, about 1917

Annie Howells Fréchette, 1919

Achille and Annie with their
son Howells and daughter Marie-Marguerite,
about 1922

Annie and Marie-Marguerite
with Howells' sons William Dean Howells and Van Derck
in San Diego, California, about 1934

Annie Howells and Achille Fréchette

Early Years:
Ohio and Canada East

The American state of Ohio and the Canadian province of Quebec are not very frequently associated in thought or imagination, and would not ordinarily be thus associated in any broad survey of nineteenth-century social developments. Both regions, it is true, originally formed part of New France: French explorers, fur traders, soldiers, and settlers were at one time almost as active on the Ohio and Miami rivers as they were on the St Lawrence; but by the early nineteenth century the French fact remained in the middle western states only in the vestigial forms of occasional place-names, or in straggling *canadien* boatmen and guides, or in small communities of French-Canadian immigrants of republican sympathies. Furthermore, French-speaking Canada after the fall of Quebec became a tightly knit, rather introverted, and sectarian society, obsessed with preserving a kind of 'racial purity' based on religious homogeneity and fidelity to ancient traditions, while nineteenth-century Ohio is generally identifiable with the myths and actualities of progress which characterized the American frontier. But the American Middle West into which Annie Howells was born in 1844, and the district of Canada East where Achille Fréchette was born three years later, can on closer scrutiny be seen to share certain features of New World sociology and geography. It is worth speculating, furthermore, that the two main characters of the following story, although brought together largely by accidental circumstances, may have been partly attracted to each other by their recognition of similar elements in their backgrounds.

First, in the most obvious and general terms, Ohio and Canada East were both primarily rural agrarian societies, although by 1850 the first inklings of industrialism were emerging with the expansion of larger urban centres like Cincinnati and Montreal, and this economic shift was clearly reflected in the evolving significance of an urbanized middle class of small businessmen and artisans. The birthplaces and the families of both Annie Howells and Achille Fréchette virtually epitomize this shift as well as the vague rural nostalgia that inevitably accompanied it. Both were born into middle-class families, in villages which were rapidly becoming suburbs of large industrial and commercial centres. Annie, the daughter of a printer and newspaper editor, was born in Hamilton, in southwestern Ohio, near the expanding industrial centre of Cincinnati. Achille, the son of a building contractor, was born in Hadlow Cove, part of the town of Lévis, across the St Lawrence River from Quebec City.

Although born in the south of Ohio, Annie Howells spent her childhood (from the age of eight) and young womanhood in the northeastern part of the state. This region, paradoxically known as the 'Western Reserve' (it was for a time 'reserved' or held back under the control of Connecticut, after that state turned over to the federal government a large land grant on the western frontier, comprising much of modern Ohio), was for the most part made up of villages and farms. The population of the Western Reserve in the 1850s reflected, furthermore, the conflicting experiences and emotions which in all parts of North America constituted the response to an era of rapid social evolution. Basically, most of the people of the Reserve were transplanted New Englanders, would-be pioneers and frontiersmen whose migration was impelled by contemporary popular visions of westward expansion and by impatience with what appeared to be the decadent and retrogressive societies of the eastern seaboard. Yet, as is often the case in immigrant societies, by the time a generation or so had grown up on the frontier, the New Englanders of Ohio tended to become in many ways more conservative and retrospective than the society they had abandoned. As one historian of Ohio has observed: 'when New England itself was being veritably transformed by the rapid inroads of modern industrialism and of the Irish immigrant, this newer New England was still following, in the main, an agricultural life.' And this same historian goes on, significantly, to point out the similarities between this situation and the situation in French Canada: 'As Quebec was, in a sense, more like Old France than France itself, the Western Reserve was in some respects more like the land of the old-time Puritan than the region east of the Hudson.'[1]

The Howells family was not, however, of New England extraction. Annie's father, William Cooper Howells (1807–94), was born in Wales, and brought to Ohio as a child. His father had been a Quaker, and although William Cooper ultimately became a follower of the religio-mystical philosophy of Emmanuel Swedenborg, the Quaker influence was clearly reflected in a prominent tendency among most of the members of the family towards unvarying kindliness, tolerance, a graceful courtesy, and indefatigable optimism. The story of William Cooper Howells' various struggles to establish himself as a newspaper publisher, and his family's Ohio peregrinations, has been told in the several volumes of reminiscences written by William Dean Howells in old age, and by the novelist's biographers. Only the most prominent facts, particularly as they affected Annie Howells, need to be recapitulated here.[2]

When Annie Howells was born, her family was experiencing an unparalleled interval of prosperity and contentment. After several attempts at establishing himself in publishing and other business enterprises in southern Ohio, in 1840 William Cooper Howells purchased the Hamilton newspaper, which for several years prospered as the local voice of Whiggism. When the Howells family moved to Hamilton, the children included only Joseph (born 1832), William Dean (1837), and Victoria (1838). At Hamilton were born Samuel (1840), Aurelia (1842), Annie (29 March 1844), and John (1846). Within six years of their arrival at Hamilton, however, the American political scene changed drastically, and William Cooper Howells' fortunes declined. Unable to agree with Whig support of the war with Mexico, Howells became a Free Soiler, insisting in print that the war was merely an attempt on the part of southern commercial interests to extend the slave territories. A significant portion of the population of southern Ohio, in contrast to the inhabitants of the northern part of the state, derived from Virginia and the Old South, and accordingly tended to be sympathetic to the traditions and aspirations of the slave states. Howells found himself in increasing opposition to the majority; finally, in 1849, his newspaper and his affairs in Hamilton collapsed.

Annie Howells was only five years old when the family left Hamilton and so of course retained no distinct memory of the community and region which her novelist brother so lovingly evoked many years later in two volumes of reminiscences, *A Boy's Town* (1890) and *Years of My Youth* (1916). But she always retained an affectionate, sentimentalized image of the American south, an image which occasionally occurs in her fiction, and which probably derived in part from family reminiscences of southern Ohio.

Her detailed personal memories begin, however – at least as far as the written record is concerned – two years after the family left Hamilton, when William Cooper Howells became briefly involved in a Utopian communal paper milling project in a wilderness area in Greene County, on the Little Miami River, east of the town of Dayton. For almost a year the family lived a pseudo-pioneering life in a log cabin, and if the experiment proved an episode of privation, drudgery, and disillusionment for the older members of the family, it was an inevitably exciting interval for seven-year-old Annie and her brothers and sisters, including fourteen-year-old Will. Some sixteen years later, when she was trying to establish herself as a writer of magazine fiction, Annie wrote a rough draft of a story based on this 'Eureka Mills' community and discussed by letter the feasibility of her project with her novelist brother.[3] But in accordance with a pattern which was to occur more than once in their literary relationship, Annie never completed the project, leaving William to pick up the idea and develop it into a book of reminiscences, *My Year in a Log Cabin* (1893), and a novel, *New Leaf Mills* (1913).

It was in 1852, shortly after the disintegration of the Eureka Mills experiment, that the Howells family moved to Ashtabula County in the Western Reserve, where William Cooper was to take up the proprietorship and editorship of the *Ashtabula Sentinel*. At first the family and the newspaper were established in the town of Ashtabula, but in 1853 both were moved to the county seat of Jefferson, a village of some seven hundred people, which was to be the Howells family's home (although not its continuous residence) until a few years after the death of William Cooper Howells in 1894. Annie Howells here attended elementary and high school; as an excited teenaged girl, observed and participated in the home front of the US Civil War; and finally, in 1872, set out in the footsteps of her brother Will to seek her fortune in journalism and fiction writing.

The years in Jefferson while Annie Howells was growing up seem to have been relatively happy ones for the family, but they were by no means marked by economic and social stability. The *Sentinel* was a successful but not remarkably prosperous newspaper, and to supplement his income William Cooper Howells took sessional work beginning in 1856 as a clerk at the state legislature in Columbus, while leaving the management of the newspaper to his oldest son, Joseph. In 1857 his son William Dean began accompanying him to Columbus, as a legislative correspondent to various midwestern newspapers, thus launching out on his full-time professional literary career. From then on, Jefferson became 'back home' for the future novelist, a place to write to and return for occasional visits, as his pursuit of literary fame took him far afield, to Europe, and eventually to permanent settlement in New England. Accordingly, the village of Jefferson did not play a large part in the formative years of William Dean Howells; but his published reminiscences, particularly *Years of My Youth*, are a valuable source of information about the town and about the Howells family life in the late 1850s. The novelist was particularly struck by the 'Yankee' quality of Jefferson, and by the eclectic forms of religious experience to be found there, ranging from atheism to fundamentalist evangelism, obviously representing the continuing reaction against the Puritan oligarchy of New England from which the early settlers of the Western Reserve had sought to escape.[4]

But in spite of this tendency to religious liberalism, Jefferson was to some extent a rather unprogressive place, which tended to cherish its own local habits of thought and action, and to regard exceptional intellectuality with suspicion. Accordingly, the members of the Howells family, with their tincture of southern manners, their fondness for books, and with William Cooper Howells' inclinations to the relatively abstruse doctrines of Swedenborgianism, were perhaps regarded by their fellow villagers with some reserve. Although there is no suggestion in *Years of My Youth* that the family was ostracized, William Dean Howells does stress his own cultivation of solitary habits while living in the village, and mentions the local farmers who would regularly visit the Howells printing office to stare with uncomprehending condescension as the compositors went about their work.[5]

In this kind of environment, it is safe to conjecture, the bookish Howellses were probably thrown a good deal on their own resources. They were a close family, unified particularly by the strong but mild and temperate personality of William Cooper Howells, whose long obligatory absences from home during the legislative sessions seem in no way to have mitigated his children's devotion to him. A lot of the responsibility for the raising of the younger children must have devolved on the mother, Mary Dean Howells, who seems to have been a somewhat retiring but hard-working woman, who for years endured the varying course of the family's economic fortunes, while pursuing the routine of child rearing and domestic drudgery which was the inevitable lot of the middle-class housewife of her era. In recalling his mother's attitude to household chores, William Dean Howells provided a glimpse of the day-to-day routine which must have been a central part of his sister Annie's life as she was growing up in Jefferson: 'In some things she drew a sharp line between the duties of her boys and girls in the tradition of her Pennsylvania origin. Indoor work was for girls, and outdoor for boys, and we shared her slight for the Yankee men who went by our gate to the pasture with their milk-pails. That was woman's work though it was outdoor work.'[6]

But neither William Dean nor Annie Howells seems to have left much in the way of written reminiscences of their mother, who died in 1868 at the age of fifty-six. 'She was always the best and tenderest mother,' William recalled briefly in *A Boy's Town*, mentioning how she would always try to keep up with her husband's intellectual interests, as for instance, 'at night, when her long toil was over, she sat with the children and listened while he read aloud.'[7] But although Mary Dean Howells was alive the whole time that Annie was growing up in Jefferson, it is clear that the father made the greater impression on her in these formative years. Certainly her personal independence, her eager intellectual curiosity, her love of travel, and her literary ambitions all suggest the influence of her father and her older brother.

It was undoubtedly William Cooper and William Dean who inspired and encouraged Annie in her love of reading. In *My Literary Passions* (1895), William Dean speaks of a barrel filled with books collected by his father over the years and with which the teenaged son, recently inspired with a voracious appetite for reading, whiled away rainy afternoons and idle evenings during the year in the wilderness at Eureka Mills.[8] It is safe to assume that Annie eventually discovered this library, and although she seems not to have followed her brother all the way in his wide-ranging and often exotic studies in literature and languages, she had an early familiarity with some of the classics as well as the popular books of the mid-nineteenth century. A brief diary, kept when she was sixteen, contains lists of books she read in 1860 and 1861, which include *The Vicar of Wakefield*, *Jane Eyre*, *Idylls of the King*, *The Mill on the Floss*, and *A Tale of Two Cities*, as well as such ephemera as *Life in Tuscany*, *Linda: or Incidents in the Life of a Slave Girl*, *An American among the Orientals*, and fiction by the prolific popular novelist Mrs E.D.E.N. Southworth.[9]

The general atmosphere of Jefferson may also have contributed to Annie's intellectual energy, as well as to other facets of her character. Small town society in the Western Reserve, as has been seen, presented something of a paradox: in some ways, it was very conservative and traditional; in other ways, it was actively involved in the radical and progressivist social experiments which were an inevitable part of the western frontier. At a time, for example, when New England girls like the poet Emily Dickinson were attending ladies' seminaries to be instructed in music and sketching and the domestic arts along with the bare essentials of an academic curriculum, many Ohio girls like Annie Howells were receiving the benefits of radical experiments in public education. The famous *Eclectic Readers* of Ohio educator William H. McGuffey, which virtually revolutionized American primary education, were first published in the 1840s and 1850s, just as Annie Howells was receiving her schooling. The first public and coeducational high schools in the state began to appear in the 1850s, and at Jefferson High School Annie received – at least in accordance with the standards of the time – the essentials of a solid academic education.

The spread of public education on the frontier was probably not, however, so much a sign of hyperactive intellectuality as an expression of the spirit of Jacksonian democracy, and specifically the egalitarian assumption that every individual, male or female, had the right and ability to pursue knowledge as well as happiness. Frontier democracy formed a part of the Howells children's upbrining in another important way. The 1840s and 1850s were the decades in which the painful problem of slavery came to a head in the United States. Ohio was one of the states where the problem was virtually omnipresent to the population during the years leading up to the Civil War: freed slaves, escaped slaves, and slave hunters were fairly common sights in the cities, towns, and countryside of the state. Further, Ohio was split geographically in sentiment, the southern portion (where the Howellses came from) generally sympathetic to the Old South and the northern regions generally on the side of Abolition. William Cooper Howells' 'free soil' sympathies had led to the family's economic ruin in Hamilton, and during the Jefferson years he followed the general drift of liberal sentiment concurrent with the political rise of Abraham Lincoln. An even more immediate and dramatic manifestation of the impending conflict appeared to the Howells family and the inhabitants of the Western Reserve in the person of John Brown, who until 1855 lived in the Reserve, and whose son and namesake settled in Jefferson shortly after the events of Harper's Ferry. In this atmosphere of abolitionist and anti-secessionist sentiment, Annie Howells' notions of politics and society were formed, notions which for years – including many of the years of her residence in Victorian Canada – were radically republican and democratic.

Radical republicanism and the ideals of Jacksonian democracy were by no means antipathetic to the society in which Annie Howells' future husband was born and raised. In general, French Canadians of the early nineteenth century were guided by their religious leaders in deploring the atheistical French Revolution and accepting in principle an English government which guaranteed the preservation of their language and religion and indigenous social traditions. But in 1837 a long accumulation of frustration with British administrative incompetence and arbitrary authority had erupted in violent rebellion; and although the small rebellion was easily suppressed, it had provided French-Canadian patriots with a glimpse of possible achievements, including the possibility of ultimate independence and the creation of a republic on the American rather than the French model. These ideals and sentiments were very much in evidence during Achille Fréchette's youth, and were concisely reflected in the words which Achille's brother Louis reports in his *Mémoires intimes* (1900) as a rallying cry commonly heard among French-Canadian children at play as well as at political meetings: 'Hourrah pour Papineau!'[10]

The electrifying patriot and politician Louis-Joseph Papineau was virtually an object of worship among French Canadians of Louis and Achille Fréchette's generation. It was undoubtedly Papineau's liberal, republican political sentiments which ultimately inspired the two Fréchette brothers with impatience towards their own country and region and admiration for the more obviously progressive and libertarian United States. Some of their admiration for these common nineteenth-century ideals may, however, have also been derived from the example of their father. Louis-Marthe Fréchette (1811–82) does not appear to have been a very politically conscious individual, but he aspired to the rising French-Canadian urban middle class which was trying to get away from the static and stereotyped life of the habitant towards a more progressive way of life modelled on American and English-Canadian experience. Beginning from the farming village of St Nicholas on the St Lawrence southwest of Quebec City, Louis-Marthe worked by turns as a labourer, boatman, and carpenter, until finally settling in Hadlow Cove, a suburb of Lévis, across the river from Quebec City. Although illiterate, he created a prosperous business as a building contractor, and it was in the relative comfort of a fairly large house in a middle-class suburb that most of his children were born.

Achille Fréchette was the seventh of nine children born to Louis-Marthe and Marguérite Fréchette. With the terrible infant mortality often typical of the period, only four of these children reached maturity: Louis (born 1839), Edmond (1841), Achille (13 October 1847), and Louis-Napoléon (1850). In addition, Louis-Marthe and his wife

adopted four children, including an orphaned niece, a Scottish boy
some years older than their son Louis, and two Irish girls orphaned by
the dreadful typhoid epidemics which struck the immigrant ships in
Quebec harbour in 1847.[11] This home environment, reflecting a combination of exceptional Christian charity and material prosperity,
ought to have been a distinctively happy one, but Achille's memories of
his childhood in Lévis were not entirely pleasant. From a very early age
he suffered from acute eye trouble, a problem which persisted
throughout his life. Compounding this physical problem was the severe emotional shock of his mother's death when he was only six years
old. In an old-age reminiscence of his childhood, Achille significantly
combined these physical and emotional problems in an image of his
mother as a beautiful, saintly nurse, ministering to his distress:

Mes souvenirs me représentent une femme assez svelte, encore dans la tren-
taine, avec une abondante chevelure dont les châtoyantes ondulations pre-
naient à la lumière des reflets ambre et or. Je la vois, quand je m'éveille, tard
dans la nuit, silencieuse, éclairée d'une bougie, penchée sur de la couture après
la longue journée d'un travail qui ne diminue jamais ... Tout ce travail, comme
je le retardais, moi, aux longues heures où un mal d'yeux persistant m'imposait
d'atroces douleurs! Et comme sa tendresse m'entourait de sympathie et de
soins dans la chambre noire à laquelle mon mal me condamnait![12]

By contrast, Achille's memories of his father were tinged with a significant ambivalence. From the remote perspective of old age, Achille
could recall the charitable and industrious qualities of his father's
character:

Il contribua largement à l'érection du collège et du couvent de la Pointe-Lévy.
Doué d'une honnête ambition en même temps que d'un esprit ingénieux,
pratique, capable d'embrasser et resoudre des problèmes complexes, notre
père ne tarda pas à s'assurer le succès et l'aisance dans des entreprises de plus
en plus considérables de travaux d'utilité publique, tels que construction de
bateaux, de ponts, quais, docks, et jetées, dans les ports de Québec, de Sorel, et
de Montréal.[13]

But if Louis-Marthe Fréchette was industrious and generous, he was
also inclined to express those qualities of joylessness and moral severity
which were often part of the Calvinist-like Jansenist Catholicism common in nineteenth-century French Canada, with its strong emphasis
on the dichotomy between flesh and spirit, its insistence on the con-

tinual acknowledgment of sin, and its pessimistic assumption of the elusiveness of earthly happiness.

To make matters worse for young Achille, within months of his mother's death his father took a second wife who proved not entirely sympathetic to her predecessor's children. These impressions of his father's severity and his stepmother's uncongeniality form the gist of a memoir of his home life which Achille wrote to his fiancée, Annie Howells, in 1876: 'Now, although a man of certain talents, my father together with my step-mother are uneducated people. Poor father did not know what harm it is to let a child hear only of his deficiencies. I don't think *she* cared. First I came to hate her and dread father, then to lose my affection for him, as he would never show me any. *Never* have I had a word of friendly conversation with either of them until two years ago.'[14]

His two older brothers, Louis and Edmond, were unfailingly kind to him, and Achille must often have observed or followed them as they indulged in the various games and pranks which Louis later chronicled in his *Mémoires intimes*. But Louis and Edmond were departing to begin their secondary school studies as boarding pupils at the Quebec seminary just about the same time that Achille was beginning his primary education at the Collège des Frères des Ecoles chrétiennes de la Pointe-Lévy. Sensitive and diffident, Achille found life at the college, as he later told his fiancée, 'a second edition of my house life': 'As I would never receive any sympathy from above at home, I grew very distant towards those whose circumstances I imagined to be superior to mine ... My successes at school did not do enough in the way of reaction. Beside, my estrangement from superiors, which, I suppose, had gradually averted my own father, alienated many a professor from me.'[15]

But Achille's school years, at least when seen from the mellow retrospect of old age, seem to have had their pleasant side. A sonnet published in *Le Souvenir* in 1921 recalls an anecdote from his early years at school, and provides a glimpse of a somewhat dreamy and shy but likeable child and his appreciation of a kindly, indulgent teacher:

Souvenir d'Enfance

A la cher frère Chrysostome
Le petit écolier disait dévotement
Son pieux chapelet en se rendant en classe.
Mais, quoi, n'a-t-il pas vu dans le buisson d'en face
Un merle disparaître? Il porte apparemment

Un long ver rose à sa nichée! En un moment
Le bambin d'oublier prière et temps qui passe;
Si bien que dans l'émoi de sa futile chasse
Il aura par malheur enfreint le règlement.

Le cuisinier-portier grince des dents, agite
Sa clef, son grand couteau, puis rudement l'invite
A ne plus rentrer tard; sinon il est perdu!

Autre porte à franchir! Contrit, timide, il frappe
Puis entre. Le bon Frère, à qui nul bruit n'échappe,
S'absorbe dans un livre ... Il n'a rien entendu.[16]

Among the few mementos which Achille preserved from his primary school days is a first-prize certificate for *l'écriture*, awarded to him by the Frères in 1859, when he was twelve years old.[17] He was evidently an unassuming but capable student, who progressed steadily through the various academic levels with an ease which betokened a capable scholarly mind. In this academic efficiency he particularly differed from his brother Louis, who was dismissed or who voluntarily departed in disgust from several schools in succession. Louis had wide-ranging interests and a passionate temperament, and tended to be impatient with the school routine and contemptuous of the dogmatic and often incompetent teachers encountered in the French Catholic school system, a contempt which he expresses at length in his *Mémoires intimes*.

Achille was particularly fortunate in benefiting from an energetic, though short-lived, movement to revolutionize French-Canadian schools. The standard education in French Canada throughout most of the nineteenth century involved an intensive exposure to classical studies as preparation for a narrow range of professions. But – to use the words of Mason Wade's summary – 'in the 1840's there was much French-Canadian criticism of the outmoded and rigid classical program, and much support was given to the introduction of scientific and vocational training. This development was halted by the ultramontane and isolationist reaction, which became dominant in the 1860's and 1870's,'[18] but many young French Canadians growing up in the 1850s, including Achille Fréchette, reaped the benefits of radical experiments in education.

The Collège de Pointe-Lévy, where Achille received his elementary instruction, was controlled by the Frères des Ecoles chrétiennes, a teaching order which in the 1850s was particularly zealous in the cause of the new curriculum. Instead of administering large doses of Latin and Greek, the Frères offered their students courses in French and English language and literature, including exercises in translation; modern history and geography; bookkeeping; natural history and botany; and at the advanced levels, more esoteric studies in architecture, geometry, elementary physics, and music.[19] Significantly, some twenty years later, while an official in the translation bureau in Ottawa, Achille Fréchette was to engage in a vehement public argument with the Frères des Ecoles chrétiennes over their educational policies, and particularly the allegedly inferior quality of their English instruction. But there is no doubt that the future chief translator of the Canadian House of Commons derived from the Frères something of his lifelong respect for English language and literature, as well as his firm belief in the value of practical, profession-oriented education.

The college was closed in 1860, partly because of the refusal of the Frères to conform to the movement back to the traditional conception of classical education, and Achille followed his older brothers over to the Séminaire de Québec to complete his secondary education. At the seminary, he was undoubtedly exposed to some of the classical studies he had missed at the Ecole de la Pointe-Lévy. Nineteenth-century French-Canadian custom dictated that law, medicine, and the priesthood were almost the only choices for a young man bent on a professional career; so in 1865 Achille followed the example of his brother Louis and enrolled in the law faculty of Laval University.

CHAPTER TWO

Annie Howells:
Early Dreams and Ventures

When the American Civil War broke out in April 1861, Annie Howells was barely seventeen years old. In 1861, her ambitions and imagination were being profoundly stirred by the example of her brother William, who after three successful years of journalism in Columbus had set out to distant parts of the country and the world, with his economic and literary future apparently assured. The previous year, he had toured New England and Canada as a correspondent to two Ohio newspapers, and had had the exciting encounters with some of the aging literary giants of Boston, Cambridge, and Concord which he was to describe nostalgically forty years later in *Literary Friends and Acquaintance*. Now, just as the Civil War began, he was rewarded for his writing of a campaign biography of Abraham Lincoln by an appointment as American consul at Venice.[1]

'How I wish I could see you today,' the seventeen-year-old wrote her brother a few months after his establishment in the consulate at Venice; 'I dreamed of being in Venice a few nights ago, and I was with you looking at the sun setting. It was one of the grandest sights I ever saw.' 'O how I wish,' Annie continues in the same letter, 'I could go away over the "dark blue sea" to roam through merrie old England ... and sail down the Old Rhine, and look at myself in the silvery lake[s] of Switzerland and gaze on the mountains reaching to the clouds.'[2] So far, Annie's travels from Jefferson had been limited to Columbus and Bowling Green, Ohio, where she visited relatives and had a few adolescent flirtations while no doubt making the most of these small breaks in routine to imagine herself a much travelled and exotic woman of the world after the manner of the heroines of the popular romantic fiction she was fond of reading. Her reading and daydreams and tentative

travels had already inspired her first ventures into literature: among
the mementos she preserved from her girlhood is a list, probably
written about 1860, of 'plots for short stories suggested by songs,'
including an unfinished rough draft of a story entitled 'Mistress Prue.'[3]
The words of the song suggest the tone and style of this early foray into
fiction:

> I'm in love, sweet Mistress Prue,
> Sooth I can't conceal it;
> My poor heart is broke in two,
> Only you can heal it.

These were rather unimpressive literary beginnings, but it was from
a not dissimilar point of departure that her brother William had embarked on a promising career of journalism and consular service. What
William could do, Annie decided, she could do also, and she was
resolved not merely to take the easy route of publication in the family-
owned *Ashtabula Sentinel*, even though William had himself taken this
route by publishing some of his poetry and an apprentice novel in the
Sentinel. Annie achieved her first literary success with a now unidentifiable 'scriptural acrostic' in an equally unidentifiable but apparently
sectarian publication called the *Bugle*. This achievement soon provoked the following reaction from William: 'I think if I were you, I
would not write any more scriptural acrostics for the "Bugle." I don't
like to see my sister's name printed as that of a "friend and fellow-
worker" of the Bugle-blowing people ... You ought to escape into a
story, and then send me the manuscript to see what can be done.'[4]
William, accustomed to apply the genteel ideals of the New England
literary establishment to his own writing, tended from the first to be
rather sternly critical of Annie's efforts, an attitude which from time to
time over the years was to be a source of slight friction between them.
But, in spite of this mixed response, William enthusiastically envisaged
his sisters making their mark in literature. When Aurelia, two years
older than Annie, wrote a book review for the *Sentinel*, William in
praising her efforts commented with an uncharacteristic lack of mod-
esty: 'I think our whole family has genius – that you girls particularly
have genius. You might all write. Why couldn't you, as well as the
Brontes?'[5]

Of course, during these years, thoughts of literary careers and other
idealistic ambitions were inevitably subordinated to preoccupation
with the national crisis. Between 1861 and 1865 Annie spent much of

her time, like millions of Americans on the home front, avidly following the war news and the appalling casualty reports, while perhaps
doing her small part in bandage making, fund raising, and socializing
with furloughed or wounded soldiers. But it was a tedious and frustrat-
ing existence for a young girl with dreams and ambitions of the great
world to which her author-brother now belonged. In a journal kept
sporadically during the 1860s she recorded her feelings in rather
stilted but apparently sincere rhetoric:

Up to this time my journal has been filled with the progress of the war and *en
verité* there is so little passing in my life that is worth noting that it is in a fair way
to be used in the same way. And yet what more could I expect to happen to me
than to thousands who have lived before me. The same daily monotonous life I
lead; made up of hope, despair, joy, sorrow, realization and disappointment ...
There are some who cling fondly to the past and turn and gaze back into it long
after it *is* the past, while I am ever looking into the future, and what it will bring
forth.[6]

Annie seems to have done very little in the way of literary composition during the war years, but she did embark on a semi-literary project
which undoubtedly distracted her from her boredom and her vague
thoughts of an indefinite future, by giving her a sense of the historical
momentousness of the present. As part of her war effort, and in
accordance with what was apparently a widespread wartime custom
designed to bolster Union troop morale, she exchanged a series of
friendly letters with various Union soldiers on active duty. Annie's side
of these epistolary flirtations has not survived, but she saved some of
the soldiers' letters, and they present a grimly matter-of-fact image of
the routine hardship and almost hysterical patriotic zeal which characterized one of the bitterest and bloodiest civil wars in history.[7] Annie's
resolutely cheerful temperament probably glossed over these dark
glimpses of bloodshed, or she may have absorbed them unthinkingly
into the prevailing sentimental-patriotic rhetoric of the time, but they
probably made enough impression on her to contribute some years
later to the inspiration for one of her best short stories, 'The Chances of
War' (published in *Harper's*, 1881).
    The war, which affected countless Americans in the form of sudden
and violent bereavement, left the Howells family relatively unscathed.
Annie's older brother Samuel was with the Union forces from 1863,
but he suffered nothing worse than the usual camp sicknesses. The
most severe wartime tragedy for the family was the death from

diphtheria of Annie's eighteen-year-old brother John in the spring of 1864, while he was away at school in Cleveland. John was only two years younger than Annie, and the loss of this good-natured, handsome childhood playmate was a shock very intensely felt. It was also probably during the war years that the full proportions of another family tragedy were materializing: Henry (born 1852), the youngest of Annie's brothers, was showing signs of mental retardation, apparently as a result of brain damage from a childhood accident. He was to require virtually full-time care provided over the years mainly by his sister Aurelia, with occasional help from Annie.

But in most respects the Howells family of Jefferson found themselves reasonably contented and optimistic as the Civil War drew to a close. William Cooper Howells' legislative clerkship at Columbus had ended in 1858, but the family had survived on the small income from the *Sentinel* and had even managed to find the means for brief holiday excursions. In the spring of 1865 Annie and her father and her recently demobilized brother Sam travelled to Columbus to celebrate the approaching return to national peace with a month of visiting, sightseeing, and theatre-going. The city, like the nation, was clearly in a state of crucial transition, as Annie indicated when she reported under the same date in her journal this incongruous juxtaposition: 'Last night we went to hear Artemus Ward lecture on his "Life among the Mormons"; he was very funny – and quite handsome ... On our way home we passed by 50 or 60 paroled Union prisoners. They were from Libby prison at Richmond and were a ghastly looking set – with their hollow cheeks and sunken eyes.'[8]

But Annie was by natural temperament too optimistic to dwell long on the national tragedy and its aftermath. With the war virtually over she, with millions of other Americans, could turn most of her attention once again to personal concerns. And at the moment, with her twenty-first birthday approaching, she had to make some definite decisions about the future course of her life. Marriage was an inevitable possibility for an attractive young woman; in Columbus, as well as at home in Jefferson, she was involved in the usual social relationships with various eligible young men. One incipient romance was apparently carried far enough to be coyly reported to brother Will, who responded good-naturedly, if somewhat pompously: 'I hope, my dear little girl, we shall be at your wedding, and that the blood-red blossoms of war will all have fallen dead before your orange-blossoms are gathered.'[9]

In 1862 William had gathered his own orange blossoms with Elinor Mead, a girl of prosperous and cultured family from Brattleboro, Vermont, whom he had met two years earlier while she was visiting relatives in Columbus. Now at the end of the Civil War Howells was preparing to resign his Venice consulship and return to the United States with his wife and two-year-old daughter Winifred, to devote himself full-time to the profession of literature. After a couple of false starts in free-lance writing and editorial work in New York and Boston, the young author of a recently published travel book on Venice settled down in the spring of 1866 to the position of assistant editor on the pre-eminent and trend-setting *Atlantic Monthly*.

Annie Howells must have found her brother's brilliant success both inspiring and intimidating. Resolutely she set to work on her own apprentice efforts in short fiction, while contributing occasional features and space fillers to the *Sentinel*. But she must have ruefully reflected that as a woman she could hardly expect to achieve a consular appointment or a senior editorial position, or even to see the great world of Europe and new England. So when an invitation came from William and Elinor to spend an extended visit with them, Annie's dreams of travel and literary achievement blossomed anew, and she embarked on the long train trip from Ohio to Massachusetts in January of 1867.

Exuberant, sociable, garrulous young Annie Howells took staid literary Boston and Cambridge by storm. Far from being overawed by the many semi-legendary literary giants who exchanged visits with her brother and sister-in-law in their suburban Cambridge home, Annie very soon gathered to herself a brilliant group of admirers. The aging Henry Wadsworth Longfellow was delighted with her sprightly conversation, desolated when she went back to Ohio in June, and sent her an inscribed copy of his *Courtship of Miles Standish*. The elder Henry James took her to the Natural History Museum, and perhaps overwhelmed her with his immense and frequently obscure transcendentalist erudition. At a party at the James house she met 'Harry James [i.e., Henry James, Jr., the novelist], who is going to be a great author ... Arthur Sedgwick, a writer for the NA Review, Hon. Richard H. Dana, ex-gov. Washburn, Professors Child and Wright ...' The distinguished Professor Francis J. Child of the Harvard English department became her devoted admirer, and invited her to attend concerts and other university functions with him. She also made a firm friend of Hjalmar Hjorth Boyesen, the Norwegian-born poet, novelist, and scholar. Boyesen found Annie an intelligent and congenial interlocutor in literary discussions, which he continued with her by letter after her return home to Ohio.[10]

As a climax to her conquest of literary New England, while she was staying in Cambridge Annie had her first story accepted by a national magazine. The brief story, 'Frightened Eyes,' was a ponderously moralistic tale for children, with a lack of thematic focus which was to be a frequent defect of her fiction. Beginning as a narrative of the Civil War, it develops into a temperance story, and concludes with rather gratuitous horror as 'little Jimmy' sees his drunken father accidentally drown. 'Frightened Eyes' was accepted by *Our Young Folks*, a juvenile magazine issued by Ticknor and Fields, publishers of the *Atlantic Monthly*, so her brother's editorial positon may have contributed indirectly to Annie's success. But this possibility by no means detracted from the delight of the experience. 'Oh how I hope I can make a name for myself,' Annie exclaimed to her journal. 'Dear Will was almost as pleased as I was.'[11]

Back in Ohio in June 1867, Annie found herself more restless and more ambitious than ever. In accordance with an arrangement which was to prevail for years between them, Annie began sending her stories to William in Cambridge, who would attempt to place them in appropriate periodicals. The last quarter of the nineteenth century was the golden age of magazine publication in the United States, and there were many opportunities for the persistent individual of passable literary skill. But as when William was starting out in the 1850s, the centre of literary America was still in Boston, and as long as Annie remained in Ohio she could hope to make her mark only with the help of her brother. William, however, still sternly demanding in his critical standards, would not offer his sister unqualified encouragement. Committed to the realist principle of the importance of writing from personal experience, William rigorously condemned Annie's flights of romantic or melodramatic extravagance. In the fall of 1867, she sent him the rough draft of 'Incidents and Scenes for a Child's Story Founded on Life at Eureka Mills' which he approved though advising her to revise further; shortly thereafter, she sent him a romantic sea story.

I have read your story [William wrote], and admire its pretty fancy and invention, but it is not near so good as the first, because you have left the solid ground which you knew for regions in which you could only guess your way. You wrote successfully of wild life in a cabin, because we had all led such a life;

but you've not been at sea, and I think that the fairies died some years before you were born. You may be sure that the imagination can deal best with what is of most familiar experience. I want you to celebrate incidents of our western life, no matter how rude or how thinly disguised, and then you cannot fail ... I imagine your eyelids getting a little red at this plain talk, but you know that it comes from the best, though the bluntest of brothers.[12]

Unfortunately, Annie tended to ignore or follow only partially her brother's editorial advice. The Eureka Mills story remained unrevised and unfinished, while she went on writing according to the prevailing conventions of popular 'domestic sentimentalist' fiction, with its stress on happy or moralistic endings, unusual or incredible characters, and artificial 'literary' dialogue. Another child's story, 'Jaunty,' was placed with the children's magazine *The Little Corporal* in 1868, and Annie went on contributing occasional news features and fillers to the *Sentinel*, but for a while it began to appear that her incipient literary career would languish. She toyed briefly with the idea of teaching school in Columbus or Cleveland, but schoolteaching was still an underpaid profession which young women – Annie was now twenty-four – tended to enter temporarily until they could escape into marriage. As she confided to her friend Mrs William H. Smith of Columbus, wife of a journalist friend of her father's, marriage was far from her thoughts at the moment.[13]

Finally, Annie resolved to commit herself to the literary profession. She was particularly determined to persist in the light of the fact that with the emergence of new social standards and customs in post-war America, more and more women authors were appearing not merely on the pages of children's and women's magazines, but in the *Atlantic* and *Harper's* as well as in the daily newspapers. It is worth noting, for instance, that her brother was about to publish, in 1869, the first story of the brilliant New England local colour author, Sarah Orne Jewett. Annie also decided, perhaps in the light of William's rather cool encouragement (or perhaps recalling his beginnings in Columbus), to pursue her career in the burgeoning journalistic milieu of her native Middle West. Resolving to combine her literary ambitions with her love of travel, and making good use of her social contacts, she wrote to William H. Smith, recently established as editor of the *Cincinnati Chronicle*. Receiving a favourable reply,[14] Annie engaged to produce a series of travel letters concerning Lake Erie ports. Although this crucial year 1868 was darkened by the death of her mother in November, the correspondence to the *Chronicle* marked the beginning of Annie's

notably successful newspaper career. Within the next few years she
added to her list of regular patrons of her free-lance articles the
Cincinnati Commercial, Cleveland Herald, Chicago Tribune, Buffalo Courier,
and *Ohio State Journal,* as well as her father's *Ashtabula Sentinel.*

In the summer of 1870 Annie made another visit to New England,
and for the first time extended her travels into Canada. Her brother
William, after having published two very successful books of European
travel, was preparing to combine the travelogue genre with fiction for
the book that was to become *Their Wedding Journey* (1872). Having
decided to give his new work a North American setting, William
wanted to refresh his memory about northern scenery and resorts. At
first Annie resolved to accompany her brother and sister-in-law only on
the railway trip to Niagara Falls, from there to return immediately to
Boston, so she took only a small handbasket of clothes with her, but at
the Falls, William and Elinor persuaded her to come on the steamer
trip with them through Lake Ontario and down the St Lawrence. This
impromptu excursion became the germ of another of Annie's abortive
literary projects to be successfully adapted by her brother. Shortly
afterward, she began planning a story tentatively titled 'A Tour in a
Basket'; but as repeatedly happened, the realist process of creating
fiction out of the apparently insignificant elements of personal experience seemed to elude or intimidate her. The story was never finished;
and the idea was picked up and developed by William into his second
novel, *A Chance Acquaintance* (1873).[15]

The fictional Kitty Ellison of *A Chance Acquaintance,* as William insisted, is based on Annie Howells only in 'the surface and striking
points.'[16] In 1870, Annie at twenty-six was some five or six years older
than Kitty; and although Annie still had a good deal to learn about the
world, the vivacious young westerner who had been able to hold her
own unselfconsciously with such eminent personages as Longfellow
and the elder Henry James was quite distinct from Howells' naive
heroine. The love story of *A Chance Acquaintance,* furthermore, is
entirely imaginary. The 'fierce democracy' of Kitty Ellison's
background, however, and her consequent resolution not to be intimi-
dated by the priggish Boston Brahmin Miles Arbuton, undoubtedly
suggest something of Annie Howells' character. And some of Kitty's
fresh, spontaneous reactions to the grandeur of the Saguenay scenery
and the quaintness of Quebec antiquity probably reflect Annie's reactions.

On the whole, Annie seems to have been entirely charmed by her
glimpses of Canada at Kingston, Montreal, and Quebec City, but obviously she could have no intimation of her eventual involvement with

the country. In the autumn of 1870 she was back in Jefferson, working to expand her free-lance journalism contacts and on the constant look-out for a permanent staff position with a newspaper or magazine. Full-time women journalists were still a relatively new idea in the United States – most periodicals preferred to retain women only for occasional assignments, to review books, or write social notes and sometimes travel articles – but Annie Howells was not an individual to be discouraged by social custom or tradition. Encouraged by her father, whose Swedenborgianism and liberal social views accepted an enlightened conception of the status of women, Annie looked into the possibility of employment in Columbus and Cleveland, and as far away as Chicago and Boston.

Finally, in the summer of 1872, Annie's long-sought literary success seemed about to be achieved. She had a short story accepted by the *Galaxy* magazine of New York, and was engaged as book reviewer to a Chicago newspaper, the *Inter-Ocean*. The story, 'Fireworks,' as William accurately observed in a letter, marked a vast advance over any of her previous attempts at fiction.[17] She was still not strictly heeding her brother's advice to write from personal experience, but she was finally avoiding the simple melodramatic conclusion, and learning to convey an impression of the drama and irony inherent in the ostensibly simple and familiar situations of life. The story involves a chance encounter between a young woman and a young man on a train, an encounter which quickly and predictably blossoms into love, but which ultimately disintegrates when the girl later accidentally burns a paper bearing the young man's name and address, thus losing track of him for ever. The plot includes just the combination of unextraordinary detail and accidental circumstance which William Dean Howells liked to develop in his fiction, as he had done, for instance, in a similar way in *A Chance Acquaintance*, which is also about a love affair aborted by apparently trivial but decisive events. Also like her brother, Annie carefully builds up an impression of reality through an accumulation of convincing descriptive detail, as in the heroine-narrator's reference to her 'crushed hat, dusty face, and ill-arranged hair,' or the parade of train passengers filing down the aisle, looking hopefully for empty seats.[18]

On the whole, 'Fireworks' suggests that Annie was on her way to becoming a passable literary disciple or imitator of William Dean Howells. 'How you did strike out in your love story!' her sister-in-law Elinor exclaimed after reading 'Fireworks' in manuscript. 'It seems to me to be immensely ahead of anything you ever did before; and soon it will be *Miss* Howells as well as *Mr.* Howells in the magazines.'[19] But as in many similar situations involving aspiring creative artists with established or famous relatives, Annie perhaps hoped for something more than being merely the literary disciple or protégée of her brother. Although she willingly accepted his help in various ways, she always refrained from asking him to use his editorial influence directly on her behalf: 'I do not intend ever to embarrass you by offering anything to the *Atlantic*,' she told him a few years later, 'although I know it will be next to impossible to make a reputation except as a contributor to it.'[20] With opportunities in the magazines thus limited, Annie continued to look to the newspapers as the primary source of opportunity for her writing career. In the magazines she could never be more than the sister of William Dean Howells, but in the newspapers – especially the radical, democratic, frontier newspapers of the Middle West – she might make a name for herself as a pioneering woman journalist. Thus the opportunity with the Chicago *Inter-Ocean* was particularly encouraging. After making arrangements for room and board with a family known to her father, in August 1872 Annie set out, with high hopes, for Chicago.

CHAPTER THREE

Achille Fréchette:
en face du grand voyage

By a coincidence which must later have afforded opportunity for pleasant speculation between the two people involved, Annie Howells arrived in Chicago just ten months after Achille Fréchette had left the city. Chicago had been the climax of the first stage in Achille's career, after the successful completion of his studies in law, and after his apprentice efforts towards a literary career in Quebec City. In 1868, just as Achille was completing his legal studies, Laval University announced a poetry contest calling for submissions of epic or lyric poems on the theme of the Canadian martyrs. Achille had been continually writing poetry during his years at the seminary and law school, and although he had had nothing published as yet, he was encouraged by the example of his brother Louis, who at twenty-nine was a regular contributor to the leading French-Canadian newspapers and magazines, the author of a volume of poems, *Mes Loisirs* (1863), and according to widespread opinion one of the most promising young poets in Canada.

Thus encouraged by ambition and example, Achille submitted to the contest a long poem entitled 'Les Martyrs de la Foi au Canada.' His submission did not win, but it was given honourable mention, and was chosen in preference to the first-prize poem to be published in the *Revue canadienne*. Most exhilarating of all was the praise bestowed on Achille's 'Martyrs' by Pamphile Le May, the eminent poet and scholar, just recently risen to national distinction as the translator of Longfellow's 'Evangeline.' In a public address on the subject of French-Canadian literature, Le May included some remarks on the new generation of young Quebec poets: 'Que je me garde d'oublier la phalange des poètes qui s'avance radieuse! C'est Achille Fréchette, c'est Poisson, c'est Beauchemin! Les uns, comme Achille Fréchette, Beauchemin et Poisson, émaillent nos revues de perles charmantes.'[1]

Achille's 'Martyrs' was indeed a promising poem according to the French-Canadian critical standards of the day. A mélange of historical narrative, religious meditation, and nature description, it incorporated virtually all the popular sentiments and preoccupations of the nationalistic school of poets which had been flourishing in French Canada since François-Xavier Garneau published his *Histoire du Canada* in 1845–8. The narrative details in the poem are undoubtedly derived from Garneau, with possible supplementary inspiration from the American historian Francis Parkman, whose *Jesuits in North America* had just been published in 1867. Indeed, Parkman's history may well have been the inspiration for the entire poetry competition. The agnostic New England historian's sceptical and rationalistic (albeit generally laudatory) interpretation of the seventeenth-century Jesuit missions had seriously angered the Catholic scholars of Laval, who were anxious to encourage among their young countrymen the traditional pious and mystical view of the martyrs.

In any case, Achille Fréchette's poem is strictly orthodox in sentiment, giving not the least indication of the author's own ultimate tendencies toward religious scepticism. In slightly less than three hundred lines, he presents a general tribute to the sublime natural landscape and flourishing civilization of his native country, goes on to identify 'le sang fécond des Martyrs' as the seed from which the country has grown, gives an impressionistic and anecdotal account of the struggles and deaths of the seventeenth-century missionaries, and concludes with a series of semi-incantatory stanzas in praise of the martyrs.

In technique as well as theme, the poem is entirely conventional. Its anapestic tetrameter – four-foot, twelve syllable lines, with the accent on every third syllable – was a common rhythm used by such French romantic poets as Victor Hugo and Alfred de Vigny, then at the height of their popularity among French-Canadian poets. The lush invocation of nature and the North American Indian primitivism of the opening stanzas recall the work of the Irish poet Thomas Moore, to whom Achille alludes in his poem and whose 'Canadian Boat Song' was enormously popular in French Canada in the mid-nineteenth century. The relentless evenness of rhythm in Achille's 'Martyrs' sounds somewhat tedious, but accords with the general emphasis in nineteenth-century French poetry on the musical quality of verse. At times, the musical rhythm and sensuous imagery of 'Les Martyrs' combine to achieve noteworthy lyrical and dramatic distinction, as in this description of the fatal winter journey of de Nouë, the first Jesuit to die in the Canadian missions:

> C'est l'hiver. Des monceaux de glaces entassées
> Couvrent du Saint-Laurent les rives délaissées;
> De gros flocons de neige obscurcissent les airs;
> La nuit descend du ciel, nuit hâtive et profonde,
> Un pauvre prêtre, seul, sur la berge qui gronde
> S'avance à pas tardifs dans des sentiers déserts!

But the tone of the poem often becomes strident and the imagery becomes extravagant, as the poet affects an artificial and redundant religious zeal:

> Martyrs, votre vertu n'a jamais eu d'égale:
> Comme elle votre gloire, étoile sans rivale,
> Luira dans l'avenir!
>
> Allez cueillir au ciel le prix de vos conquêtes;
> Ici, des nations inclineront leur têtes
> A votre souvenir![2]

Still, as a poem on a prescribed topic by a twenty-three-year-old author who would inevitably be deferential to a powerful cultural establishment, 'Les Martyrs de la Foi au Canada' was an auspicious beginning. Soon afterward, *La Revue canadienne* accepted a second poem from him, 'Quand on fait son droit,' a light satire on the pedantry and tedium involved in the study of law.[3] Earlier in the summer of 1868, Achille had had published in *Le Journal du Québec* a brief poem entitled 'Juillet,' a wry commentary on the tendency of the hot Quebec summers to bring out on the city promenades some peculiar specimens of high fashion. In accordance with Pamphile Le May's prophecy, Achille seemed destined to follow his brother's footsteps toward poetic fame.

Actually, his two poems on law and high fashion revealed a talent for satire which might have provided a means of escaping the rather derivative nationalistic-lyrical strain of poetry represented by his own 'Martyrs' and by most of his brother's work. But the influence of Louis and current French-Canadian poetic trends proved much too powerful for him, and Achille ultimately settled into the position of a minor poet producing occasional lyrics of distinction, within the prevailing poetic rhetoric of his time.

In 1868, as throughout much of his early life, Achille's ambitions and achievements were dominated by the example of his brilliant and successful brother. He and Louis in early manhood looked very much alike: they were both of short stature, rather inclined to stoutness, comparatively fair complexioned, and with round faces, set off in Achille's case with thick spectacles compensating for his chronic eye weakness. As Louis had done, Achille was pursuing the study of law with a view to a career in journalism, the acceptable professional outlet for a nineteenth-century French Canadian with literary ambitions. The era of Canadian Confederation was, as has been noted, an extremely nationalistic time for French Canada: a time of heated political debates in the periodical press as in the streets and homes, of intensive analysis of the French-Canadian past and present, and of various attempts to establish definitively the framework of a native Canadian culture.

In the lives and works of young poets like the Fréchette brothers, of the generation to which Pamphile Le May applied his prophetic praise, the tenor of the age tended to be expressed in two complementary ways. On the one hand there was a strong sense of community, and of pride and ambition on behalf of the French-Canadian identity and its prospective contribution to world culture. On the other hand there was a sense of indignation directed against the memory of the English conquest and the continuing domination of English-language culture in North America. Related to this indignation was a general sense of dissatisfaction, of suspicion that both the US melting pot and the British-designed Canadian Confederation were threats to French-Canadian national survival. Among the more radical young Quebec intellectuals, this situation tended to provoke an intense rebellious spirit, and at times a rather artificial and dramatized self-projection of the French Canadian – especially the French-Canadian artist – as an outcast, alien, and rebel.

This type of nineteenth-century *canadien errant* was epitomized in the life and writings of young Louis Fréchette. Of rebellious temperament from childhood, Louis had been expelled from several schools in succession, had been reluctant to settle into any one profession or locality, had gone to New York state, had returned and completed his law degree, had worked sporadically for one French-language newspaper after another, and now in 1868 was editing a francophone newspaper in Chicago. More than most French-Canadian intellectuals of his generation, he was a confirmed admirer of French civilization and culture; his professed idols were the itinerant French romantic poets Lamartine and Hugo, and his interest was

particularly caught by the later period of Hugo's life and career, spent
in exile. By the same token, he continued to look back admiringly to the
career of Louis-Joseph Papineau, another exile, although by the 1860s
Papineau was a distinguished elder statesman who had made his peace
with the English-Canadian establishment. Like Papineau, Louis
Fréchette came to have a guarded admiration for the American republic and its respect for individual freedom, even though he recognized
that it represented potential assimilation of ethnic minority groups
such as French Canadians.[4]

In temperament, Achille Fréchette was not really like his brother.
Rather quiet and reserved, patient and hard-working, he had more of
the careful rationality of the scholar than the spontaneity of the poet.
But the dramatic figure of the exile, the poet-rebel, and the impas-
sioned Francophile presented by his brother could not fail to appeal to
young Achille, and within months of his call to the Quebec bar he was
making plans to join Louis in Chicago.

The extent of Achille's imaginative involvement in the romantic
myth of the *canadien errant* is suggested by an unpublished poem
entitled 'A mes amis, à la veille de mon départ pour les Etats-Unis le
jour de mes vingt-deux ans, 13 octobre, 1869.' The second of the
poem's three stanzas is as follows:

> Maintenant que, dans le monde,
> A voguer nous apprêtant
> Timides, nous sondons l'onde,
> Nous interrogeons le vent,
> En face du grand voyage
> A travers notre avenir;
> Amis, donnez du courage
> Au premier qui va partir.
> A l'heure où l'âge me donne,
> O Dieu qui nous réunis,
> Je te bénis! tu me donnes
> De bons amis![5]

The sea-voyage imagery – which is rather incongruous, considering
that he is setting out for the American Middle West – the self-
dramatization, and the fervently sentimental celebration of friendship,
all reflect the conventionally romantic poetic idiom in which both
Achille and his brother Louis were working in this early stage of their
careers.

Louis, however, with his rather erratic school career behind him, and his impatience with current political and social institutions in Canada, seems to have been not quite as anxious as Achille to sentimentalize the past. In a sonnet from these Chicago years, 'A mon Frère Achille,' Louis urges his brother, as if in answer to Achille's poetic invocation of the friends of his youth, to think of their early lives only as preparation for greater things to come:

> C'est l'avenir, vois-tu, qui frappe à notre porte;
> Laissons le passé fuir avec ce qu'il emporte;
> Oublions s'il fut triste ou s'il fut caressant ...[6]

But minor differences in their respective attitudes aside, these two poems clearly reflect the rather narcissistic Byronic pose of these two young French Canadians in their self-imposed exile.

From a more comprehensive historical perspective, Louis and Achille Fréchette appear not as Byronic exiles to a remote and barbarous frontier, but as minor characters in one of the most massive dramas of urban migration in history. Chicago in 1869 was the fastest-growing city in North America: a focal point for the accelerated westward migration following the Civil War, and also in the vanguard of post-war US industrial expansion, the city jumped in population between 1850 and 1870 from thirty thousand to an astounding three hundred thousand people. Immigrants poured in from all directions: more than half the newcomers came from Europe, especially from Ireland and Germany, along with thousands of native-born Americans from the eastern states, a small stream of former slaves from the South, and perhaps two thousand Canadians of French extraction.

The main economic impetus in Chicago was provided by the huge network of railroads which connected the wheat and cattle lands of the west with the cities of the east, and provided the crucial medium of transportation for the continuous stream of immigrants and freight passing through the city. Chicago was also becoming an important lake port, as well as a manufacturing centre to rival the older centres of New England. Everywhere he looked, when he arrived in the fall of 1869, Achille Fréchette must have seen construction, as the commercial section of the city stretched out for miles along Lake and State streets in increasingly impressive brick and steel buildings, usually of only four or five storeys since the elevator was yet to be developed, and often featuring elaborate pseudo-Gothic cornices and tall arched windows. There was poverty as well as enormous wealth in the Chicago of 1869: within sight of the mansion of millionaire industrialist William B.

Ogden were row upon row of jerry-built shanties for the workers in the stockyards and the meat-packing plants. But this kind of incongruity, which was later to stir the social conscience of America (as when, for instance, twenty years later William Dean Howells was to speak out in defence of the Chicago Haymarket rioters), seemed in 1869 to be the epitome of the 'American dream'. The shanty dweller of one year might be the millionaire of the next, and two newly arrived young French-Canadian immigrants might shortly become moguls of the newspaper industry.[7]

There was room, at least, in this sprawling and bustling city for a modest French-language newspaper. Events in Chicago actually seemed to move too swiftly for the famous us 'melting pot' to work successfully: national groups managed to preserve their ethnic identities, especially when they congregated in their own exclusive neighbourhoods, and a francophone newspaper could do much to promote the cultural survival of the French Canadians of Illinois. The newspaper which Louis had established in the previous year was called *L'Amérique*. Aggressively Francophile and republican, its editorial policies stressed the importance of cultural solidarity within the Franco-American community of the Middle West, and advocated the continuation of such Canadian cultural institutions as the Saint Jean-Baptiste Society to serve as focal points for French political and social aspirations. Under the editorship of Louis, *L'Amérique* also urged the expansion of cultural affinity with France, as a means of compensating for the ponderous American anglophone influence.

Achille, junior member of the editorial staff and somewhat less political than his brother, probably concentrated his efforts on news features and cultural contributions such as book reviews. For at least six months the journalistic venture must have provided him with an exhilarating introduction to his presumed life's work, although there must also have been difficult moments. Louis, still as restless as ever, divided his time and attention among his editorial duties and various literary and political ventures: recently excited by the theatre, he wrote a play and an opera, while involving himself in the local and national politics of his adopted country. In the summer of 1870 he had one of his occasional bouts of homesickness and departed for Canada, leaving his inexperienced brother to cope as best he could with the editorial work.

While Louis was in Canada, the Franco-Prussian war broke out. The war inevitably called out Louis' Francophile sentiments with renewed vigour; his republican principles seem not to have been bothered by the fact that France was currently under the despotic imperial rule of Napoleon III. After publicly asserting his solidarity with France at the French consulate in Quebec City, he rushed back to Chicago with the intention of using *L'Amérique* to rally Franco-American emotional support to the cause of France. To his horror, he discovered that in his absence the backers of *L'Amérique* had replaced him with a French-speaking Swiss of German ancestry, who was defending the Prussian cause in the newspaper. The francophone readers of *L'Amérique* were predictably annoyed, and one by one subscriptions disappeared.[8]

Louis angrily resolved to turn his back on both *L'Amérique* and Chicago, and in the fall of 1870 he and a Canadian friend descended the Mississippi to fulfill a long-standing ambition to visit the exotic remnant of France in the United States, New Orleans. Within a few weeks, however, he was back in Chicago, where after securing appointments as Canadian correspondent to two American newspapers he set out for his native country.

Achille, meanwhile, either resigned from *L'Amérique* or was dismissed as an economy measure some time early in 1871, and until the fall of that year he was connected with the real estate business in Chicago. The nature of this connection – whether as speculator or clerical employee, or both – is not clear, but he seems to have made enough money during his stay in the American West to invest in one hundred and sixty acres of Nebraska farm land in early 1873.[9] His career in Chicago came to an abrupt end in the fall of 1871 when on the evening of 8 October erupted the great fire which devastated more than four square miles of the city, destroying virtually all of the commercial centre. *L'Amérique*, which had been floundering financially, perished both as a building and as a business enterprise, like much of the real estate which was the current source of Achille's income. The calamitous fire brought out the traditional fighting spirit of Americans, and real estate offices along with many other commercial enterprises were open for business in temporary quarters within days of the conflagration; but Achille Fréchette apparently decided that he had had enough of the new midwestern metropolis.

He was not, however, prepared to return to Canada; in spite of the tribulations of *L'Amérique*, and in spite of his dramatic observation of the boom-and-bust economic conditions which prevailed on the western frontier, Achille still preferred the American republic to the Canadian Dominion. 'I have sworn off allegiance to the queen,' he was to write his fiancée some five years later, 'and in '72 declared my intention of becoming an American citizen.'[10] His anti-British republicanism is also reflected in a poem dated just four days before the Chicago fire and published two weeks later in *L'Opinion publique* of Montreal. 'L'Irlande: Romance' expresses the poet's empathy with the

> Terre féconde et poétique
> Où le dernier des troubadours,
> Embrassant sa harpe celtique
> Mourut en chantant ses amours,

and goes on to lament the Irish patriots expelled from their native land:

> Hélas! douloureuse agonie,
> J'ai vu, les yeux de pleurs voilés,
> L'ange de la blonde Hibernie
> Qui pleure ses fils exilés.[11]

'L'Irlande' thus suggests that in spite of the disillusioning experiences he had encountered in the United States, Achille had by no means put aside the self-dramatized image of the *canadien errant* which he had derived from Louis. In his imagination, he was still an exile like the Irish patriots.

The young Canadian exile next drifted into Nebraska, where he was briefly involved in the lumber business before joining the staff of the *Platte Valley Independent* in the town of Grand Island.[12] He remained with this newspaper from some time in 1872 until the spring of 1874, and was just about to complete the process of naturalization as a US citizen when an opportunity suddenly arrived from Canada. *Le Courrier d'Outaouais* of Ottawa had recently changed hands and the new owner, L.A. Grison, wanted Achille to join him as co-editor. In spite of his republicanism and his growing attachment to the American West, Achille decided that the Ottawa opportunity was too attractive to pass up. The small *Platte Valley Independent* really offered limited prospects for a francophone writer; on the whole, opportunities for advancement in the journalism of his native language were greater in his own country than in the United States. So his Nebraska farm was placed in the hands of a tenant, and in March 1874 Achille set out for Canada.

A more comprehensive factor in Achille's decision than the immediate prospect of employment in francophone journalism was undoubtedly the new Canadian political situation. The Conservative government of Sir John A. Macdonald had collapsed with a resounding crash in November 1873 under the weight of the squalid and grimy scandal over bribes and kickbacks in the building of the Canadian Pacific Railway. The massive popular support for the Conservatives, derived particularly from the magnetic personality and reputation of Sir John A., disintegrated virtually overnight. The Liberals under Alexander Mackenzie found themselves with the heady prospect of holding governmental power indefinitely against a totally discredited opposition. A general election in January 1874 found the Liberals with one hundred and thirty-eight seats to the Conseratives' scant sixty-seven.

The Liberals, furthermore, had much solid French-Canadian support, inspired particularly by the efforts and personalities of such promising young members of parliament as Wilfrid Laurier, a distant cousin of the Fréchettes and a friend of Louis'. Louis had returned to Quebec in 1871 to throw himself energetically into Canadian politics, and after two unsuccessful provincial candidatures he had carried the riding of Lévis in the Dominion election of 1874. The *Courrier d'Ou-taouais* was an aggressively Liberal paper, and it seems likely that Louis, with his growing reputation in journalism and literature, had successfully recommended his young brother for the vacant position. In any case, Achille arrived in Ottawa to join the new wave of Liberalism which seemed to promise a new era for French Canada and for the country as a whole.

In March 1874 the masthead of the *Courrier d'Outaouais* began to read 'Grison, Fréchette, & Cie., éditeurs propriétaires,' indicating that Achille had invested money in the venture. The *Courrier* did not use bylines, but part of Achille's contribution can probably be discerned in occasional book and periodical reviews and in the increased attention to literature noticeable from that time.

The main business of the paper, however, was politics; and events in 1874 offered plenty of opportunity for the pursuit of this business. Throughout the spring and summer of that year there were frequent editorials advocating amnesty for Louis Riel, the fiery métis rebel of Manitoba who had been elected to parliament in 1874 while facing criminal charges for his part in the Red River Rebellion, and who was now a refugee in the United States. There was, predictably, continuous praise for the policies of the Mackenzie government and unfavourable comparison with its Conservative predecessors. There was also, in April 1874, a very flattering editorial portrait of Wilfrid Laurier, probably written by his young cousin Achille Fréchette, praising a recent speech of Laurier's in the House of Commons.

But Achille's career with the *Courrier d'Outaouais* was to be relatively brief; in Ottawa a new and unexpected field of opportunity opened up to him. In the years immediately following Confederation, the Canadian civil service had inevitably proliferated because of the continuous political and social development of the new nation. The Mackenzie government declared its intention to develop a refurbished, nonpartisan civil service, and although their ideals in this direction were slow to be realized – government employment continued indefinitely to depend to a greater or lesser degree on party patronage – there was an immediate movement toward a larger, more stable, and better-paid network of public employees. Somewhat disillusioned by his few years' experience with the vagaries of newspaper publishing, and lacking his brother's essentially adventurous outlook on life, Achille was attracted by the possibility of stable, well-paid employment. In July 1874 he detached himself from the *Courrier*, and possibly with the patronage of Louis or Wilfrid Laurier or both, he entered the civil service as a clerk of the House of Commons committee on Agriculture. Early in 1875, recommended no doubt by his journalistic experience and his fluency in English gained during his years in the United States, he became an assistant in the Commons translation bureau. In this bureau he was to remain for the next thirty-five years.[13]

CHAPTER FOUR

Chicago, Boston, Quebec

Annie Howells' journalistic career in Chicago was even briefer than Achille Fréchette's. Arriving in the city in August 1872 during the post-fire reconstruction and economic resurgence, she was undoubtedly excited by the spectacle of apparent prosperity and solidity as the inhabitants sought to avoid a repetition of the catastrophe by replacing many of the old wooden structures with new buildings of brick and stone. But any such impressions of affluence were illusory, for in the summer of 1872 Chicago and the United States as a whole were on the brink of a severe economic recession.

Having settled into her boarding place, Annie turned to writing for the *Inter-Ocean*, being assigned particularly to magazine and book reviewing. Her brother William, who in 1871 had been promoted to the full editorship of the *Atlantic*, sent her a continuous stream of encouragement in her journalistic efforts, while urging her not to neglect the writing of fiction. 'I hope that in going to Chicago,' he wrote, 'you'll keep story writing constantly in mind. Do the best you can at your newspaper work, but keep trying something higher all the time, for you have a faculty in fiction that is quite rare.' 'I'm glad to know that you're to notice the magazines, for I know you'll do it well. But you mustn't devote yourself so entirely to the newspaper as not to be able to write stories and sketches.'[1] In spite of William's encouragement, however, Annie managed to find little time for the writing of fiction. Some time during her stay in Chicago she did turn out a story called 'A Windy Night,' which she placed with a local magazine, the *Hospital Bazaar*; but most of her time was taken up with her work for the *Inter-Ocean*, and with occasional reports on Chicago to be sent back home for publication in the *Sentinel*.

Annie was apparently one of the first full-time women journalists in Chicago.[2] The idea of women in career journalism was new enough in 1872 to touch off a semi-comic exchange of letters between herself and William when the *Inter-Ocean* editors assigned her working space in their office – an unheard-of measure, as lady contributors to periodicals always did their writing at home. Hearing of this arrangement, William – who was by temperament rather fastidious, particularly in the matter of social proprieties – seems to have sent off an unfortunately worded expression of disapproval, to which Annie immediately and indignantly responded, assuring him of her competence to look after her own conduct and reputation. 'The letter gave me a headache,' she wrote to her sister Aurelia; 'I told Will that if I gave up my room at the office I would give up my place too, for I *could not* write at my boarding place.' But William promptly apologized: 'I never knew you to do a silly thing, and I merely hated the publicity of your having a room at the office,' and the incident was soon forgotten.[3]

William received further assurance of the respectability of his sister's position from their old family friend William Henry Smith, who in 1873 moved to Chicago as head of the Western Associated Press syndicate. 'I immediately went to the *Inter-Ocean* office,' he informed William Dean Howells, 'and found Annie ensconced in her editorial chair – able and dignified.'[4] Annie's professional position with the *Inter-Ocean* was, however, to prove frustratingly brief. In the spring of 1873 the newspaper was sold, the usual reorganization and staff changes ensued, and after less than three months in the position of literary editor, Annie was once again out of a job. She may have looked about for other newspaper work in Chicago, but the economic recession was now in full swing, and frontier boom cities like Chicago with their high rate of speculative activity were severely affected. There was nothing to do but go back home, and in April Annie was in Jefferson once again.[5]

Annie was now twenty-nine years old, and had still not made her mark in her chosen career. At least she was far behind her brother William, who at twenty-nine had written three books and was assistant editor of a leading national magazine. But Annie was not one to brood on invidious comparisons or thoughts of failure; ever optimistic and ambitious, she was soon making plans for her next literary venture. Having been disillusioned by her experience of Chicago, she turned once again to thoughts of pursuing her career in New England, the traditional literary Mecca where her brother had done so well. Making use of her brother's recommendation and his extensive editorial contacts, she proposed to find permanent employment in Boston or, failing that, to establish herself as New England literary correspondent to various midwestern newspapers. All through the summer of 1873 she wrote letters of application, and William wrote on her behalf, although he advised her that 'I confess that I should be sorry to have you take another place on a newspaper, for it seems to me that would be simply delaying your real work, which is something higher.' 'You are too good for any but the best newspaper work, and I think your true calling will be story-writing.'[6] However, Annie persisted in her plans, and although she was unable to secure a permanent staff position, in October she set out for New England as correspondent to the *Cincinnati Commercial, Buffalo Courier, Ohio State Journal, Cleveland Herald*, and the New York *Hearth and Home*.[7]

Accompanied by her sister Aurelia, who planned to spend the winter with her, Annie took room and board in Boston and settled down to her journalism. Her writing in this stage of her career is epitomized by an article, 'Literary Matters in Boston,' which she wrote in November and sold to the *Hearth and Home, Cleveland Herald*, and *Buffalo Courier*. The article begins by acknowledging the courage of American publishers in the current economic recession, then strides quickly and efficiently through the typical literary pot-pourri which tended to descend on a nineteenth-century reviewer's desk, particularly in the Christmas gift-book season. In a long review of the current issue of the *Atlantic*, she includes a favourable notice of the concluding serial chapter of a novel by her friend H.H. Boyesen, and the latest of a series of European travel articles by Henry James.

On the whole, Annie's newspaper review work in Boston reveals a talent for the synthetic generalization and popularization appropriate to this kind of writing, and suggests that in spite of her brother's emphasis on the importance of persisting in fiction, her main talents were in journalism. The highlight of her free-lance career in Boston came in February 1874, when she sold to the *Chicago Tribune* a witty but dignified interview with the visiting British cleric and novelist Charles Kingsley, an interview which received the ultimate accolade of being plagiarized by the *New York Express*. In reporting the plagiarism to her, William offered further misguided discouragement: 'If I were you, I wouldn't do any more interviewing. You can't dignify it, it's poor business after all.'[8] In spite of such comments, however, Annie persisted with her newspaper writing, making a modest income to keep herself and Aurelia comfortable in Boston over the winter of 1873–4.

In the meantime, back home in Jefferson, events were moving toward a whole new stage in Annie Howells' life. For several years her father had been trying to use his long record of support and service to the Republican party to acquire a consular appointment from the administration of Ulysses S. Grant. Finally, in the spring of 1874, he was named us consul at Quebec City. This was not the most desirable of assignments, in comparison to some of the more picturesque and more remunerative European consulships such as his son's wartime assignment to Venice; but the salary and fees at Quebec promised to support William Cooper Howells and his family in modest fashion. The *Sentinel* was placed in the hands of his eldest son, Joseph, who had been virtually exclusive editor and manager of the enterprise for some years, and early in June Howells with his daughter Victoria and his son Henry set off for Quebec. Annie and Aurelia decided that it would be practical to join the family in Quebec, where Annie could carry on with her free-lance writing, and where they could live considerably more economically than in Boston.

Before setting out for Quebec, Annie got in touch with an old Ohio friend of the family, Whitelaw Reid, who was now editor of the *New York Tribune*, and enlarged her economic prospects with a promise from Reid to publish a series of her travel letters on Canada. A whole new vein of journalistic subject-matter was opening up for her to supplement her literary writing, and Annie was quick to take advantage of it. Although it is frequently assumed that there was no widespread popular or literary interest in Canada among nineteenth-century Americans, the fact is that the more picturesque regions of the country were enormously popular as tourist resorts, and many of the visitors wrote up and published their travel impressions. Henry Thoreau, in his *Yankee in Canada* written in 1850, refers to fifteen hundred fellow tourists who were taking advantage of a special railway excursion fare to Montreal and Quebec.[9] As rail and lake steamer facilities expanded in the next twenty-five years, tourist traffic correspondingly increased, along with the literary coverage of this traffic. The frontier humourist Artemus Ward visited and wrote about Quebec in 1865, as did E.L. Godkin (editor of the *Nation*) in 1868, and the young novelist Henry James in 1871, along with many lesser known contributors to newspapers and magazines.

American interest in Canada – or at least, French Canada – had been especially aroused by Francis Parkman's series of histories of New France which began publication in 1865 and appeared in sporadic volumes over the next thirty years. Among American authors influenced by Parkman and by an intrinsic interest in Canada was William Dean Howells, whose first two novels, *Their Wedding Journey* and *A Chance Acquaintance*, involved American tourists in the province of Quebec. Howells' *A Chance Acquaintance*, just published in 1873, with its love story set against the picturesque background of Quebec City, was enjoying tremendous popularity in the United States, and journalists were eager to exploit feature articles on the various settings made familiar to Americans by the activities of the fictional Kitty Ellison and her companions. So in very quick succession Annie was able to place such articles as 'Quebec: First Impressions of the Ancient City' (*Cleveland Herald*, August 1874), 'Dominion Notes: Quebec as an Intimate Friend' (*New York Tribune*, October), 'Quebec' (*Chicago Tribune*, November), and 'Canada in Winter,' (*New York Tribune*, December).

French Canada, and particularly the city of Quebec, in the 1870s had an irresistible appeal to anyone with an eye for the picturesque. The old walled city with its eighteenth-century fortifications, its small but architecturally elaborate churches, its narrow cobbled streets filled with horse-drawn calèches, presented an image which was as close to European antiquity as it was possible to come in the comparatively recent civilization of North America. And the French-speaking inhabitants, many of them still affecting vestiges of colourful peasant costumes derived from seventeenth-century France and speaking a language which was almost unchanged from the era of Louis xiv, suggested to visiting Americans an older, less hurried, more tranquil civilization than their own.

To a visitor with a wide experience of Europe, there might seem something artificial and self-consciously quaint about the place. Henry James complained of a rather theatrical quality to the city's attempts to imitate the old world: 'it appeals to you so cunningly with its little stock of transatlantic wares that you overlook its flaws and lapses and swallow it whole.'[10] And William Dean Howells felt that the city, like Canada as a whole, presented the impression of suffering from confusion of identity as its customs and institutions wavered indecisively among affinities with imperial Britain, pre-revolutionary France, and modern America.[11] A particular source of antipathy for many visiting Americans was the ubiquitous and archaic Roman Catholic church, which was the most prominent sign of what seemed French Canada's perverse refusal to commit itself to the enlightened and progressive modern world of Protestant-inspired industrialism and individualism. One feature, however, which went a long way towards compensating for the alleged defects and ambiguities of French-Canadian society was the natural setting of Quebec City 'perched on its mountain of rock, washed by a river as free and ample as an ocean-gulf, sweeping from its embattled crest, the villages, the forests, the blue undulations of the imperial province of which it is warden.'[12]

The Howells family established their combined living quarters and consulate in a rented house on Hamel Street, centrally located in the old walled city or 'upper town,' in a neighbourhood of narrow cobbled residential streets between the Hôtel-Dieu and Laval University. The environment, with its picturesque impressions of European antiquity and with the various cultural ambivalences of a highly stratified bilingual society, must have demanded considerable adjustment from a family of small-town midwestern Americans. Inevitably, they tended to gravitate socially toward the local consular community, becoming particularly intimate with the representative from Spain, the suave and cultured Count Premio-Real. The open and convivial Howellses were easily approachable, however, to any and all visitors. 'The consul's residence,' wrote Quebec cultural historian James Le Moine, 'was soon renowned for its musical and literary activities.'[13] A more detailed glimpse of the consulate in the first year of William Cooper Howells' tenure is available through a contemporary article in the *Springfield Daily Union* (Mass.), by 'Gondi de Retz' (Boston journalist and scholar Arthur Gilman):

Any reference to Quebec at the present time would be imperfect without mention of the United States consul there, Mr. William Cooper Howells, who is always to be found at his official residence, near the ramparts, and is ready to do much more than his simple duty for any of his countrymen in need. Aided by his accomplished daughters, he makes his weekly receptions and the other gatherings in his pleasant drawing rooms, most agreeable. There he brings together many who stand high in official circles, and men of letters of France, Spain, England, Canada, and America.[14]

As one of the accomplished daughters of the consul, Annie undoubtedly did her part in the various social responsibilities of the household; but throughout 1874 and 1875 her time was much taken up with literary activity. In addition to her regular newspaper correspondence, she had finally committed herself, some time early in 1874 while still living in Boston, to the ambitious project of writing a novel. All through the spring and summer she devoted whatever time she could spare to the project, until finally in October she was ready to make a final draft, and in accordance with her long-standing custom in her fiction writing, she sent it off to her brother for his opinion before submitting it for publication. As she might have expected, William was relentlessly frank in his criticisms of stylistic infelicities, improbabilities of plot and character, and particularly of what he considered to be a gratuitously melodramatic conclusion; but he deferred to her insistence that the manuscript should be submitted without further revision. The necessary prerequisite to book publication of a novel in the United States at that time was serialization in a prominent national magazine. Annie's work was thus submitted to the *Galaxy*, which had published her story 'Fireworks' two years before. To her great delight, the novel was accepted late in November, and scheduled to begin in the magazine toward the end of 1875.

Annie Howells' novel, *Reuben Dale*, is on the whole a very promising first attempt in the late nineteenth-century realist mode of American fiction. The story involves an American girl, Agnes Morgan, who marries a widower some twenty years her senior, and who subsequently falls in love with a handsome young army officer named Reuben Dale, thus precipitating a situation with predictably tragic results. Thus baldly summarized, the plot sounds rather melodramatic, which in many respects it is; but the author is careful to build up a convincing image of social and psychological reality. Her heroine is not the spiritless, simpering ingénue of popular fiction, but like her creator (and here Annie must have particularly remembered her brother's constant injunction to write from personal experience), she is an intelligent and experienced woman in her late twenties. The army officer is no moustache-twirling cad, but a sensitive if somewhat egotistical young man driven to impetuosity and mistaken judgment by years of lonely service on the western frontier. The wronged husband is a particularly noteworthy success of characterization: vain and garrulous to the point of tedium, he also reveals a competence and conscientiousness within his own limited sphere of experience which his wife gradually comes to recognize and respect.

The action, too, is carefully motivated and logically developed. Because social conventionality has become second nature to persons of his background, Reuben Dale imagines himself to be falling in love with an unmarried friend of Agnes; and it is only with mounting self-revulsion that he gradually realizes he has been unconsciously displacing his affections. Similarly, Agnes begins to recognize her sexual attraction to Dale very slowly and reluctantly, and tries to repress it by avoiding Dale and devoting herself to the active appreciation of the acknowledged merits of her husband. The novel ends, furthermore, with the potentially effective irony of the husband's complete ignorance about his wife's infatuation.

The conclusion of the novel, however, gives way to forced and violent melodrama. Gathering all her strength for one final gesture of renunciation, Agnes sends her would-be lover away from her out into a storm; Dale is struck and killed by lightning, and Agnes is driven insane by the shock. In addition to this flamboyant conclusion, the novel suffers from frequent infelicities of diction and irrelevancies of dialogue and narration. The story begins very slowly and confusedly, with a poorly integrated summary of an unhappy love affair in Agnes's youth; and her friend Jenny is later identified, in a development of no consequence to the main plot, as an aspiring novelist. As the story approaches its gratuitously violent climax, the language becomes stilted and the sentence structure clumsy: 'As he went out into the storm which was upon them in its fury his heart beat quickly with the pain which filled it, and yet through it the certainty that she would love him again when the horror of the present was over was the comfort which sustained him ... "She cannot cease to love me; her heart will still be mine, even as mine will be hers, and until death I will love her." '[15]

However, some elements of the narration are extremely well done, such as the semi-comic characterization of Agnes's husband-to-be, whose fantastic notion of courtship conversation is a lugubrious monologue on the death of his first wife:

Many times during the month he had shocked her almost beyond forgiveness by his crudeness, his lack of sentiment, and his practical manner of treating subjects which she had always thought of with reverence and utmost delicacy. But she had forgiven him many times, always finding some good to balance the bad. She had even pardoned him in her mind (for he never dreamed he stood in need of mercy) after he had spent a whole afternoon entertaining her with a minute description of the last illness and death of his wife. From the recital he seemed to derive a certain pleasure, which she could not understand, unless it was that the remembrance of his unceasing kindliness to her and the profusion with which he had spent his money upon doctors filled him with self-commendation.

'I should like to have you see the monument I have erected to her memory,' he had said in conclusion; and encouraged by her expression of the pleasure which the sight would give her, he described it at length, not, it is true, with the technicalities of an architect or sculptor, but quite vividly enough to give her an idea of its proportions and grandeur, as he did, not omitting to name the sum he had paid for it.[16]

On the whole, the infelicities of style, plot, and character in *Reuben*

Dale suggest that the novel was in need of at least one further thorough revision. As a work of late nineteenth-century fiction, it compares favourably with a great many less memorable efforts published in the magazines and in book form. In one particular respect, *Reuben Dale* is worthy of special note. Departing courageously from contemporary Anglo-American moral standards, the author treats the subject of marital infidelity. Adultery had, of course, been used as a literary theme many years earlier in a classic American work of fiction, but Nathaniel Hawthorne's *The Scarlet Letter* had approached its subject through the half-lights and indirections of romance, which in the author's famous words deals with 'a neutral territory, somewhere between the real world and fairy-land, where the Actual and the Imaginary may meet.'[17] The post-Civil-War American realists, who professed to deal mainly with the concrete and tangible surface of reality and with the familiar or recognizable elements of human experience, generally tended at first to avoid such sordid sexual themes.

The European realists, particularly Balzac and Flaubert, had dealt with adultery, but European explicitness on this subject had little influence in the United States until the appearance of Tolstoy's *Anna Karenina*. The extent of Annie Howells' literary audacity is fully evident when it is recalled that *Anna Karenina* was just being written as *Reuben Dale* was published, and did not appear in English until 1885. A comparison of a relatively slight magazine piece like *Reuben Dale* with a masterpiece of Russian realism is easily dismissed as ludicrous, but certain parallels of plot and character are worth noting in order to appreciate some of the social and artistic ramifications of the common theme of these two works. The male lovers in both novels are young army officers; the disrupted marriages are between a young woman and an aging husband. Both novels end in exaggerated violence: Reuben Dale's death by lightning is comparable to Anna Karenina's destruction under the wheels of a locomotive. What these parallels indicate, of course, is that both writers, in spite of their realist affinities, had recourse for certain aspects of their novels to standard devices of melodrama: an army officer is often a proverbial roué, errant lovers are traditionally punished by a grimly violent nemesis. If Tolstoy rises much further above these conventionalities than Annie Howells does, his recourse to them still indicates that both writers, in dealing with a controversial theme, recognized the moral demands of their respective reading publics. Only by casting their fictional transgressors in familiar forms and by subjecting them to violent punishment could they hope to get away with treating the subject of adultery at all.

If *Reuben Dale* is thus seen as a tentative development of some of the insights and observations subsequently brought to fruition by the master of nineteenth-century European realism, the response of William Dean Howells to his sister's novel appears in a particularly suggestive light. By 1885, when an American edition of *Anna Karenina* was published, Howells' conception of the comprehensive moral and social relevance of realistic fiction had developed far enough that he could admire Tolstoy's treatment of passion and pronounce his novel 'a wonderful book.'[18] But in 1874 his theories still had serious limitations, especially as far as the selection of subject matter for fiction was concerned. 'I could wish,' he wrote Annie after reading *Reuden Dale*, 'that you had chosen some simpler and wholesomer face of human nature, which would also be fresher.'[19] This reservation about his sister's choice of subject-matter significantly prefigures Howells' famous appeal to his fellow novelists in America 'to concern themselves with the more smiling aspects of life, which are the more American.'[20] It also recalls the fact that in much of Howells' own fiction the determination to deal only with 'smiling aspects of life' frequently takes the form of an apparent reluctance to deal with sexual problems.

In his own first novel, *Their Wedding Journey*, he had deliberately defied the popular penchant for novels about conflict in love by creating a fictional anatomy of a happy and successful marriage; but it was not until 1882 that he could bring himself to write the logical corollary to this early paean to love and marriage, a novel about marital strife and divorce. His divorce novel, *A Modern Instance*, reveals, furthermore, almost exactly the same weakness that he complained about in *Reuben Dale*. 'I should say,' he wrote Annie, 'that with the ending [of *Reuben Dale*], the story was a failure. It is violent and feeble at the same time, and I strongly advise you to invent some other denouement. To have Dale struck by lightning and Agnes go mad is a mere *coup de théâtre*, to which you ought not to resort.'[21] Yet in his own *A Modern Instance* Howells resorts to the ploy of having his errant husband – an alcoholic and irresponsible journalist who eventually divorces his foolish young wife – killed by an irate reader of his newspaper. The shooting is not quite as flamboyant as the lightning-bolt death of Annie's hero; but Howells' novel shows that he also could not avoid the obligation to dispense violent punishment to those who flout the sanctity of marriage.

But there is a definite risk of implicitly attributing more literary value to *Reuben Dale* than it actually deserves. If Annie Howells' instincts in the treatment of her subject were at least as good as her brother's, and if the novel is ahead of its time in its choice of theme, it is still at best only a promising attempt which indicates that in time the author might have become a minor contributor to the late nineteenth-century realist tradition in America. But if *Reuben Dale* does reflect such a possibility, it is particularly unfortunate that Annie never again attempted to write a novel. Her abandonment of the longer literary form, with its heavy demands of time and sustained concentration, might be explained by the fact that fairly soon after writing *Reuben Dale* she found herself with the prospect of a full-time occupation as wife and mother.

But it is also possible that her brother's criticisms of her most ambitious literary project discouraged her from making a second attempt. By 1875, William Dean Howells was the author of three highly successful novels, and as editor of the *Atlantic* was rapidly becoming the most influential arbiter of literary matters in the country. Annie seems to have depended a great deal on his example and encouragement; and without his approval, she may have felt it pointless to go on. Another probable factor in her decision to give up novel writing was the disappointing public reception of *Reuben Dale*. In spite of its controversial theme, it apparently evoked no significant reaction either from reviewers or from the reading public; and it was virtually consigned to oblivion when the eligible publishers unanimously declined to bring it out in book form.

In any case, after the publication of *Reuben Dale* she turned her attention back to short story writing and feature journalism. Her next prominent literary success was a short story accepted by *Scribner's Monthly* in October 1875 and scheduled to appear the following May. The story, 'Le Coureur des Bois,' was, however, a significant contrast to the novel. From the contemporary social realism of *Reuben Dale* she turned to the historical romance, with a tale of love and adventure set in seventeenth-century Canada. The immediate inspiration for 'Le Coureur des Bois' was the latest volume of Francis Parkman's epic history of New France, *The Old Regime in Canada* (1874), from which Annie took the epigraph for her story.

It is interesting to note that 'Le Coureur des Bois' seems to defy almost every principle of the realist creed as pronounced and illustrated by William Dean Howells: instead of taking its material from contemporary life, it looks to the past; instead of relying for its action on the probable and ordinary course of human experience, it depends on unusual events and strained coincidence; instead of accepting the logic of events so as to convey an impression of the irony of real life, it relies on a contrived and artificial happy ending of the sort common to the so-called 'domestic sentimentalist' fiction of the nineteenth century. Instead of speaking a recognizably colloquial language, the characters use a strained diction full of 'thees' and 'thous' which apparently pretends to be a literal translation from the French. It is tempting to conclude that Annie deliberately wrote 'Le Coureur des Bois' as an ironic response to her brother's criticisms of *Reuben Dale*, especially in view of the fact that *Scribner's* was under the editorship of Josiah Holland, one of the main proponents of the romantic and sentimental school of fiction in nineteenth-century America, and one of the few American literary men for whom the usually congenial and tolerant William Dean Howells expressed an open dislike. But if Annie was deliberately offering an indirect rejection of her brother's criticisms of *Reuben Dale*, Howells apparently chose not to notice, and even provided his usual help towards publication by intervening for her with the *Scribner's* assistant editor, Richard Watson Gilder.[22]

But whether William approved of 'Le Coureur des Bois' or not, this story written so soon after the semi-realistic *Reuben Dale* graphically reveals the dilemma in which many aspiring fiction writers of limited ability found themselves in the late nineteenth century. The realist-romantic controversy, epitomized in the hostility between William Dean Howells and Josiah Holland, created an excruciating tension between opposing forces. On the one hand, Howells insisted that fiction should be written from experience, or at least should create a convincing reflection of the observable surface of contemporary life, a formula by which he himself had achieved considerable critical and popular recognition. On the other hand, the most influential literary periodicals, with the possible exception of Howells' own *Atlantic*, perpetuated an older romantic notion of fiction, stressing exotic settings, unusual incidents, and especially, sentimental love situations. In writing *Reuben Dale* and following it immediately with 'Le Coureur des Bois,' Annie Howells revealed her own uncertainty about the realist-romantic conflict, an uncertainty which would persist throughout her writing career. In spite of this conflict of literary ideals, however, the publication of her novel in the *Galaxy* and a story in *Scribner's* must have been satisfying experiences for Annie, reviving with renewed vigour her determination to make yet a considerable success in literature.

CHAPTER FIVE

Love and Marriage

Within months of the Howells family's establishment in Quebec, the American consulate became a popular gathering place for regular literary and political discussions, involving members of the consular community as well as a few native Canadians, especially those of republican sympathies. Among the latter, one frequent visitor during his regular sojourns in Quebec City was the well-known poet and member of the Dominion Parliament for Lévis, Louis Fréchette. During the Christmas holiday of 1875, he paid a call to his American friends accompanied by his brother Achille, also home from Ottawa on leave from his duties in the Commons translation office. It seems to have been, for both Annie Howells and Achille Fréchette, a genuine case of love at first sight. Annie had been accustomed to think of herself as a career woman as far back as 1867, when she had told her friend Mrs William H. Smith of her disinclination for various potential suitors in Columbus and Jefferson; but now she found herself romantically attracted to this somewhat short and stocky but handsome, rather quiet, and punctilliously courteous French-Canadian visitor. If Achille, on his part, thought of marriage at all, he probably assumed that he would eventually marry a French-Canadian woman of similar background to himself, perhaps someone like his brother Louis' fiancée, Emma Beaudry, daughter of a prosperous Montreal businessman. Instead, Achille found himself after one meeting utterly captivated by the vivacious daughter of the American consul at Quebec.

Some six months after this Christmas meeting, Annie and Achille sentimentally recalled their first impressions of each other: 'Do you remember [wrote Annie] the first time you called at our house? I had been out with my brother ... and as it was snowing, I came in quite covered with snow, and my hair was guiltless of "crimps." I know I was quite non-plussed at the sight of you and your brother, as I was in such an absurd plight. I wonder what you thought of me then, or did you trouble yourself to think anything?' And Achille replied: 'Do I remember the first time I called at your house? Why, I think I remember every time I have seen you. I still see you undoing your cloak full of snow by the door, disappearing a moment, come in and sit between Mr. Howells and Miss Victoria, then come near me and sprightly keep up the conversation between us both for the rest of our call.'[1]

The courtship, in the limited time of Achille's leave from his parliamentary duties, necessarily demanded haste. Between Christmas and 19 January, when he returned to Ottawa, Achille was a constant visitor at the consulate and a frequent companion to Annie in long walks, sleighing parties, and other Quebec winter activities. Throughout February and on into the spring there was a regular exchange of letters, in which 'Dear Miss Howells' and 'Dear Mr Fréchette' gradually gave way to 'Dear Annie' and 'Dear Achille.' In mid-February, Louis Fréchette sent Annie a bantering letter declaring that 'my poor brother is desperately in love with an American lady in Quebec, very pretty and highly accomplished, which constitutes a very bad case – and I am at a loss to find a proper treatment for such a dreadful disease.' Annie responded in a similar tone: 'I confess I am puzzled to know which you consider a very bad case, the "young American lady," or the melancholy state of your brother ... The only possible cure I can see is for the poor patient to describe his case fully to the young lady herself, *then* she might know of some remedy.'

But in spite of the joking, the situation was clearly becoming serious. Achille himself nervously expressed his love by letter in the same month, and without committing herself Annie gave him guarded encouragement. In their letters of the spring of 1876, they also discussed literary matters, and discovered many common bonds of interest and taste. Finally, Achille visited Quebec again, in the week of 11 July 1876. To her sister-in-law Elinor, Annie wrote of the visit:

I know you will want to hear the result of Achille's visit. He was here a week and I enjoyed his visit greatly, and like him very much better than I did before he came. Still we have not made any arrangements yet. I felt heartily ashamed of myself when I could not tell him what I had decided to do, or rather that I had not decided at all, and I told him that I'd not ask him to give me any more time for I knew it was not right to keep him waiting, but he replied that the rest of his life would simply be 'waiting' and all he asked of me now was not to refuse him. He would like to have been married this fall, but was willing to let me take my own time. He is a dear good fellow. What I most admire in him is his exquisite refinement. All the time he was here he did not do anything but what was kind and delicate, and that is saying more than I could ever yet say of any man who has pretended to love me.[2]

Like many individuals who have reached their thirties and remained single, Annie evidently had serious reservations about marriage. This particular union, furthermore, presented at least two especially difficult considerations. If she married Achille Fréchette, she would have to face the possibility of spending the rest of her life in a remote northern capital about which she knew nothing, and in a country whose political and social institutions were to some extent uncongenial to her American upbringing. Equally serious were the religious considerations: as she explained to Elinor Howells, Achille was a Roman Catholic in name only, but social and family pressures might be invoked against them either to bring about their separation or to force her conformity to Catholic church rules in the matter of mixed marriages. 'As to having him leave Canada, of course, I'd not insist upon that. He owns a house and farm out in Nebraska, where he said he could go, but I would not think of that. His salary at Ottawa is about $1,600 a year, which is a good deal, in Canada, and he is in a service where promotion is the rule.'[3] As the summer wore on, Annie began to think of an extended trip to the United States, as a possible means of putting the personal dilemma in a different and perhaps clearer focus. It was the year of the Centennial of American Independence, and like many of her countrymen, she hoped to visit the year-long commemorative exhibition at Philadelphia. This excursion could conveniently be combined with a visit to her brother Will; so early in September she set out for his summer home in Townsend Harbor, Massachusetts.

In the summer of 1876 William Dean Howells was preoccupied by concerns of his own. Not that his immense creative energy was showing any signs of waning, or that his literary fortunes were receding: he had spent most of the summer on salaried leave from the *Atlantic* at his publisher's request, writing a campaign biography of the Republican presidential candidate Rutherford B. Hayes, who was a cousin of Elinor Mead Howells, and who as president would be in a position to offer his commissioned biographer some very attractive preferment. But as the author of three successful novels and a series of very profitable stage comedies, Howells was seriously thinking of giving up the time-consuming *Atlantic* editorial duties and venturing on a free-lance writing career. In 1876, however, the United States was in the depths of the worst economic depression it had ever known, and it was not the ideal time for speculative literary ventures. Complicating these professional questions was an annoying domestic inconvenience: Howells and his family had spent part of the summer in totally unsatis-factory rented accommodation, and an accumulation of petty an-noyances had left them all rather nervous and harassed. In short, Howells was experiencing the perennial human condition of preoccu-pation with his own real or hypothetical troubles in the summer of 1876, and could only turn his attention to his sister's problems with a rather half-hearted sense of obligation.

Many years later, however, in the last published novel of his long career, Howells turned his mind nostalgically back to that Centennial summer and provided a revealing retrospective glimpse of his sister's youthful character and problems. Like Kitty Ellison of *A Chance Ac-quaintance*, the improbably named Parthenope Brook of *The Vacation of the Kelwyns* (1920) is only like Annie Howells in the 'surface and striking points;' but the imaginary portrait of a girl 'no longer in her early twenties' who visits her cousins the Kelwyns in their vacation home during the Centennial summer probably reflects something of How-ells' memories of his sister's state of mind and personality forty years earlier. 'She was so full of initiative,' Howells wrote, pretending to report what her 'critics' said of Parthenope Brook, 'as to need all the putting down you could quietly give her; in fact, her initiative might be called self-sufficiency, though that, her critics owned, was oversaying it rather.'[4]

Parthenope Brook's self-sufficiency is clearly a reminiscence of the forceful independence displayed by young Annie Howells in her free-lance newspaper career in Chicago and Boston, and her determination to be guided in matters of conduct by her own instincts rather than by outside pressures. A more specific recollection of Annie, however, may be reflected in Parthenope's romanticism. 'It was the time when youth was very much characterized by its reading,' says the narrator of *The Vacation of the Kelwyns*, going on to reveal that Parthenope had read 'a few songs of Heine' and was familiar with some Swinburne, Browning, Tennyson, and Longfellow. More significant, however, is her taste in novels: 'George Eliot, Charles Reade, Kingsley, Mrs. Gaskell and lesser sibyls, with the nascent American fictionists of the *Atlantic Monthly* school, inculcated a varying doctrine of eager conscience, romanticized actuality, painful devotion, and bullied adoration, with auroral gleams of religious sentimentality.'[5] In short, Parthenope is the intelligent sort of reader – and would-be author – who most exasperated Howells. Not that he was totally opposed to Parthenope's reading, as the sly reference to his own magazine suggests; and English novelists like George Eliot, even secondary figures such as Charles Kingsley and Mrs Gaskell, had Howells' guarded admiration for their moral sincerity. But these authors, capable of appreciating and rendering the psychological subtleties and moral complexities of realism, often had recourse to the exaggerations and simplifications of romanticism – which is exactly what Howells accused Annie of doing in *Reuben Dale*, and which she had deliberately done in 'Le Coureur des Bois.'

The conflict between realism and romance in *The Vacation of the Kelwyns* is finally resolved, however, by the marriage of Parthenope Brook to a young man of a realist cast of mind who bears a general resemblance to Howells himself. This compromise solution, with romanticism in effect united with and brought under the benevolent domination of realism, provided an ideal happy ending for a pleasantly reflective fictional narrative; but it was not easily applicable to the real-life problem of Annie Howells in 1876. During her stay with her brother, Achille paid a visit to Townsend Harbor, and William found himself liking very much this soft-spoken and cultured prospective brother-in-law. Then on 14 September, although the religious problem remained to be settled, Annie gave her suitor a definite affirmative answer. They both went on at different times to visit the Philadelphia Centennial, and early in October Annie was back in Quebec and Achille in Ottawa, happily engaged to be married the following summer.

Love and marriage were not the only concerns of Annie Howells and Achille Fréchette in 1876–7. Achille, of course, was occupied with his duties in the translation office at Ottawa. In these early years of Canadian Confederation, the House of Commons usually met only once a year for two or three months in the spring, which meant that the translators were especially busy at that time with the day-to-day parliamentary record. But when Parliament was not in session, the office still had considerable work to do, since it was responsible for the translation of all official papers emanating from the various parliamentary committees and government departments. Since the Canadian government had committed itself by the British North America Act to a thoroughly bilingual operation, the translation office was kept almost continuously busy.

Early in the spring of 1877, however, Achille found time to apply his professional talents to a labour of love, by beginning a French translation of Annie's story 'Le Coureur des Bois.' Nothing came directly of this project – he apparently did not publish the translation – but the general idea led ultimately to significant results. 'I was mentioning the fact to Louis,' Achille wrote to Annie, 'and he took to the idea of translating your brother's books on Canada. He wishes that you would ask Mr. Wm. Dean Howells for him the permission of publishing a translation of "Their Wedding Journey" and "A Chance Acquaintance" in L'Opinion Publique or other Canadian periodical.'[6] Howells proved most agreeable to the proposal, and *Une Rencontre fortuite* appeared as a serial in the *Revue de Montréal* over the winter of 1879–80. Thirteen years later, when Louis Fréchette was at the height of his fame and influence as the 'lauréat' of French Canada, he published a revised translation of *A Chance Acquaintance* as *Une Rencontre* (1893). In 1877, Louis also paid literary tribute to his brother's prospective in-laws in a sonnet 'à Miss Winny Howells,' dedicated to the American novelist's thirteen-year-old daughter, who had accompanied her aunt Annie back to Quebec to spend the winter of 1876–7, and who had totally captivated her Quebec relations and their friends with her intelligence and pleasant personality.

All in all, it was a busy and happy winter at the consulate. Annie was continuing her free-lance correspondence to various American newspapers and, in addition, had been unexpectedly offered a new and attractive literary project. In a letter to Achille, Annie described the project presented to her by the Spanish consul, Count Premio-Real: 'Just after I closed my letter last night, the Count came in to spend the evening and unfold a grand enterprise he has on hand. He wants me to write a book with him. He is to write the outline in such English as he can command, and bring it to me. I am to take it and suit it to American taste and re-write it generally. I like the idea very much. The plan is to embody the popular songs and aphorisms of Spain in a light and pleasant style.'[7]

The resulting book, ultimately comprising only proverbs, was published in January 1877 by the local Quebec firm of Dawson and Company, in a small paperbound format, with the authors identified by the pseudonyms 'Fieldat' (Spanish for fidelity) and 'Aitiaiche' (a phonetic acronym of Annie's initials). *Popular Sayings from Old Iberia* was well enough received by the press and public to call forth a second edition in April. The *Revue de Montréal* described it as 'un charmant recueil de proverbes ... choisis avec soin et avec un goût parfait, ... traduits en

anglais de façon à ne rien perdre de leur primitive saveur.' William
Dean Howells included a brief favourable review of it in the *Atlantic*,
thus acknowledging not only his pride in his sister's contribution to the
enterprise but also his own youthful enthusiasm for Spanish culture.
On the whole, *Popular Sayings* was for Annie and her collaborator a
modest but throughly exhilarating success.[8]

Annie's second ambitious literary project of early 1877 was a short
story with which she hoped to penetrate the pages of *Harper's*, next to
the *Atlantic* the most prestigious magazine in the United States. But in
writing this story, she fell once more afoul of the realist-romantic
controversy, this time in an unexpected way. Her story was a slight
epistolary narrative entitled 'A Visit to a Country House and What
Came of It,' in which a young girl on vacation imagines herself to be
involved in a budding romance with a handsome young man, only to
discover to her embarrassment that she has been grossly misinterpret-
ing his conduct and the young man has not had romantic thoughts
about her at all. It is not a very good story – there is a repelling archness
to the tone – but in the ironic ending Annie was obviously trying to
implement her brother's repeated warnings against the obvious sentimental conclusion. To Annie's surprise, however, the story was rejected by the influential *Harper's* editor, Henry Mills Alden. 'Your
story,' he wrote, 'is unsatisfactory, simply because "nothing" comes of
the visit. The reader is left in the position of the heroine, sorry that he
has visited the country house at all. I am sorry – for the story is
charmingly told.'[9] Bemused but undaunted, Annie promptly set to
work changing the conclusion, so that the young couple discover their
mutual attraction and at the end of the story are engaged to be married. Alden thoroughly approved of this version, and 'A Visit to a
Country House' was scheduled to appear in September 1877. This was
the first of many publications in *Harper's* for Annie, and an advance in
her career ironically achieved by a complete rejection of the realist
principles which her brother had for so long been urging upon her.

A romantic story involving a successfully concluded love affair probably reflected Annie's personal mood and outlook in the spring of
1877, as her own marriage approached. A date in mid-June had been
tentatively set, and the religious question was finally settled when
Achille agreed to a Protestant ceremony, to be held in the consulate.
The occasion was as happy and propitious as the bride and groom
could wish. Many of the local consular people attended, including, of
course, the Count Premio-Real. Annie's brother Joseph came all the
way from Jefferson with his wife, and on the morning of the eighteenth

William arrived from his current summer home in Rhode Island. Louis Fréchette and his wife Emma were there, and Achille's second oldest brother whom he had not seen for some time arrived from Manitoba.

Edmond, about a year younger than Louis and the constant play-mate mentioned in Louis' *Mémoires intimes*, turned out to be an unexpected highlight of the occasion. 'Tell Mr. Fréchette,' William wrote his sister the following month, 'that I fell in love with his Manitoba brother, with whom I had a long talk the evening you left.'[10] Edmond was a flamboyantly colourful character, whose life and exploits might almost have seemed indecorous to Howells, the realist chronicler of the commonplace, if they had not been so fascinating. From a very early age he had shown remarkable talent in music, art, and literature, but his main interest had been in military matters. After taking part in a militia action against the Fenians in 1866, he had joined the papal Zouaves in 1868 and had been involved in the campaign against Garibaldi. Now, in 1877, he was currently stationed in the new province of Manitoba with the North West Mounted Police, with which he had gone west a few years earlier as part of the Canadian attempt to establish law and sovereignty in the western territories. He had been a part of the contingent assigned to guard Sitting Bull, and had seen service in and around all the semi-legendary places of the Canadian West, including Fort Walsh, the Cypress Hills, and 'Fort Whoop-Up.'[11]

Edmond's presence at the wedding was a special pleasure, but the occasion of 18 June 1877 belonged of course to Annie and Achille. Following the festivities, the newlyweds embarked on a wedding journey to New England, and in mid-July were settled in a rented house at 99 Daly Street in Ottawa, ready to begin their new life.

CHAPTER SIX

Middle Years: Ottawa

The city of Ottawa in 1877 would have presented to Annie Howells Fréchette a spectacle both familiar and new. Like Quebec, Ottawa would appear – especially to a visitor or immigrant from the United States – very much a northern city: the panoramic vista from Parliament Hill, like the view from Quebec's Cape Diamond, followed a broad and winding river into an infinite expanse of dark and seemingly impenetrable forest wilderness. But if the spectator on the hill were to feel, as Henry Thoreau did on Cape Diamond, a sense of personal insignificance and impending annihilation while gazing on this relentless image of untamed nature, he could soon discover the reassuring influences of civilization by turning his gaze down to the river, where in 1877 he would see an almost constant procession of lumber barges, log booms, and industrial and pleasure craft during the seven or eight month season of navigation. All along both shores of the river, furthermore, he could discover bustling towns and villages like Hull, Richmond Landing, and New Edinburgh, as well as numerous sawmills and other small industrial operations.

Since about 1850, the Ottawa region had been experiencing steady economic expansion as a result of a gradual increase in the demand for sawn lumber, especially in the United States. The city's vital location at the junction of the Ottawa, Gatineau, and Rideau rivers made it the logical marketing and supply centre for the logging industry of the Ottawa Valley, and the nearby Chaudière Falls provided enormous power potential for the sawmills, which by 1870 were more numerous and more productive than the mills of any other lumbering region in Canada. It might have been pleasant for Annie, furthermore, to reflect that this industrial development had been largely brought about, like so much comparable development in Canada, by the energy and investment of her countrymen. In the course of the gradual decline of the logging industry in New England and the Adirondacks, the Ottawa Valley had been 'invaded' during the 1840s and 1850s by American entrepreneurs like Levi Young of Maine and E.B. Eddy of Vermont, who in the 1870s were engaged in building huge Canadian industrial and commercial empires.

The American presence in Ottawa was not, however, confined to these modern incursions of industrial capitalism; as far back as 1800 a settlement had been established at the junction of the Ottawa, Gatineau, and Rideau rivers by a group of immigrants from Massachusetts. These 'late loyalists,' so called to distinguish them from the original United Empire Loyalist refugees from the American Revolution, were followed by others, who also found it convenient to take up free land lying relatively close to New England by the simple expedient of swearing allegiance to the British crown rather than make the long trek to the American western frontier.

At the same time, however, the Ottawa region was developing a strong British element, epitomized by the famous Colonel By, founder of Bytown, precursor of Ottawa. British half-pay officers, 'remittance men' (i.e., genteel younger sons with no inheritance of land), as well as hordes of dispossessed Irish and Scottish peasants poured into Ottawa as into other parts of Canada during the early nineteenth century, until by the 1870s perhaps a third of the population of the city were from the British Isles. Also, from the very earliest period of settlement there had been a steady stream of French-speaking immigrants to Ottawa from Montreal and Quebec and the rural areas of Lower Canada. In 1877 the population of the city stood at approximately twenty thousand, of whom roughly one-third were French-speaking. The use of two languages in the city gave it a distinctive Canadian flavour to offset the Americanization of its commerce and industry.

The distinctive Canadian character of the city was most dramatically symbolized, however, in the imposing spectacle of the Parliament Buildings, rising and extending magnificently on the brow of a hill overlooking the Ottawa River. Built between 1859 and 1876, originally to serve the united province of Canada and subsequently the federated Dominion, the Parliament Buildings were an impressive example of the Gothic revival, a style of architecture which constituted in this context a visual proclamation of the country's loyalty to Westminster and the empire of Queen Victoria. The skyline of 'towers, high-pitched variegated slate roofs pierced by dormers and surmounted by ornamental wrought iron cresting and terminals' also proclaimed the northern character of the capital and the nation. The Gothic style, with its implications of a primitivistic and generally rugged instinctual way of life, was appropriate to both the Canadian geographical context and to the Canadian imaginative self-conception, just as the classical style of architecture in Washington with its invocation of ancient southern cultures was appropriate to both the geographical position and the rationalistic political assumptions of the United States.[1]

The newly married Fréchettes arrived in Ottawa only a few days after the tenth anniversary of Canadian Confederation, and Annie Howells Fréchette must have been very abruptly plunged into an atmosphere of exuberant Canadian nationalism which would contrast markedly with the atmosphere in Quebec City, where both the French-Canadian majority and the imperialist English-Canadian community were more restrained in their loyalty to the new dominion. Nevertheless, her early impressions of the city were generally favourable, as impressions of a new and bustling social and economic atmosphere usually are. Furthermore, in spite of the symbols and attitudes of British imperialism and Canadian nationalism, there was an unmistakably American element in the social milieu of the city. Before they were married, Achille had given his fiancée an account of this democratic element in Ottawa:

Ottawa is, in my opinion, at least as much democratic as Quebec or Montreal, if not more so ... Society here is composed of more or less isolated circles, formed not in view of position, but according to the congenialities of individuals or to family ties. The city is new, the population is not above twenty thousand, and the government and House officers form the better class. Although the capital of the Dominion, Ottawa can hardly be judged of according to the state of things in the American or other capitals. There are no embassies here, no very rich ministers of the Crown – one of them is a former mason, and another has married, so the story goes, a London penny show actress – most of them board or 'batch it.' The sessions of the Parliament last but two months in the year, and the senators and MP's are our guests. It is only this year, the Supreme Court is established (one of its judges is a visitor of my bachelor's rooms). You see that we are democratic enough: social distinction has had nothing to feed on yet. The governor and his wife receive every lady and gentleman without any other but personal distinction.[2]

In addition to this congenial social atmosphere, Ottawa offered at least a promising cultural milieu, as its inhabitants sought to engage in and encourage innovative activity in the arts, befitting the city's presumed obligations to set cultural as well as political standards for the nation. The widespread nineteenth-century practice of awarding civil service sinecures to deserving artists was not yet common in Canada, perhaps partly because few deserving candidates had presented themselves, but there had already been a few such cases. In most European and American countries during the nineteenth century, furthermore, individuals with legal education and/or political experience were almost invariably inclined to be artistic patrons or dilettantes, so Ottawa had more than its share of cultural clubs and circles of amateurs.

Among noteworthy individual artists whose careers were related to Ottawa when the Fréchettes first took up residence there might be mentioned Charles Sangster, author of the poetic travelogue *The St. Lawrence and the Saguenay* (1856) and other works in the manner of the English 'prospect' and romantic poets, which were earning him a brief reputation in both Canada and England. Another briefly famous poet, Charles Mair, had lived in Ottawa in 1868, and had participated in the short-lived politico-literary 'Canada First' movement, which also included the Ottawa scholar and literary historian Henry Morgan, compiler of *Bibliotheca canadensis*, the first bibliography of Canadian literature (published in 1867). The scholarly aspects of literary activity were further represented in Ottawa by W.D. Le Sueur, later president of the Royal Society of Canada, and John G. Bourinot, in 1877 a clerk in the House of Commons but later author of the influential *Intellectual Development of the Canadian People* (1882) and *Our Intellectual Strength and Weakness* (1893). The three most famous English-Canadian literary figures in nineteenth-century Ottawa, Wilfred Campbell, Archibald Lampman, and Duncan Campbell Scott, were still schoolboys in 1877, although the following year Scott was to begin his long career with the Department of Indian Affairs, and all three young poets were to become social acquaintances of the Fréchettes in the 1880s and 1890s.

As for the francophone literary scene in Ottawa when the Fréchettes arrived, several names stand out, especially among the temporarily resident members of Parliament and the civil servants who came to Ottawa after the Liberal victory of 1874. Louis Fréchette, of course, was the most prominent name in the former category, although he found little time for literary activity while Parliament was in session, and his literary career was more and more being associated with Montreal. One of Achille's fellow workers in the Commons translation office was Benjamin Sulte, who had published two volumes of poetry in 1877 but was subsequently to make his name as the author of the encyclopaedic *Histoire des Canadiens-français* (8 vols., 1882–4). Alfred Garneau, son of the famous historian François-Xavier Garneau, was chief translator of the Senate in 1877 and a frequent contributor of poems to newspapers and magazines. Also in the civil service in 1877 was cultural historian Alphonse Lusignan, author of *Coups d'Œil et Coups de Plume* (1884). In this book, Lusignan described briefly the francophone cultural situation in Ottawa during the Mackenzie administration, especially as it was centred in the *Institut canadien*, of which he was the founding president, and which attracted members distinguished in the fields of science, politics, history, and literature.[3] There was also at least one literary periodical published in Ottawa, *Le Foyer domestique*, which began publication in 1876. In its issue of 1 July 1876, *Le Foyer* had printed a poem by Achille, an elegy to a recently deceased cousin, 'A la Mémoire de Madame E.H. St. Denis, née Fréchette.'

On the whole, the Fréchettes found Ottawa a congenial and stimulating place to live. In accordance with Achille's promise, Annie found society in the city pleasantly democratic, although like a good many Americans of her time she tended to conceive social democracy in terms of movement upward rather than downward from her own position, so was pleased to find herself in a social circle which included cabinet ministers and senior civil servants. In a letter to her sister Aurelia, she reported on her New Year's callers for 1878, and the list included such dignitaries as Judge Télésphore Fournier of the Supreme Court, Minister of Agriculture C.A.P. Pelletier, Clerk of the Privy Council William Hinsworth, Alphonse Lusignan, and numerous other civil servants and members of Parliament.[4] Achille's fluent bilingualism as well as his position in the translation department had helped him from the first to cross the slight but distinct linguistic barriers which existed then as always in bicultural Ottawa, but his acquisition of a wife who was an established English-language journalist as well as the sister of a well-known American novelist undoubtedly led to a marked expansion of his acquaintance in the English-speaking community.

About the only discouraging development in the Fréchettes' early married life occurred slightly more than a year after their settlement in Ottawa, when the Liberal government of Alexander Mackenzie was defeated in the general election of September 1878. As they had come into power in a triumphal sweep over the routed forces of their Conservative opponents four years earlier, so the Liberals now found themselves discredited and decimated as a result of a convergence of factors, including the continuance of recessive economic conditions,

Canadian nationalist antagonism to Liberal policy on reciprocity with the United States, a growing antipathy to the bland but sometimes arrogant political style of Alexander Mackenzie, and the resurgent personal popularity of Sir John A. Macdonald. Almost half the Liberal sitting members went down to defeat, including the member from Lévis, Louis Fréchette.

The civil service was nominally non-political, but many public employees were in fact, like Achille Fréchette, Liberal supporters whose positions had been rewards for party service, so in 1878 many of these people were understandably nervous about their future. Their nervousness was justified, because many Liberal appointees were turned out of office; so many, in fact, that some people feared the establishment of the American spoils system, and in 1880 there was a parliamentary inquiry into the whole system of civil service appointments.[5] Achille, after some anxious waiting, found that his job was safe: although his brother Louis was out of Ottawa, he still had influential friends such as Wilfrid Laurier. Early in November, however, Annie was lamenting to her father and sisters that Achille had been passed over for promotion and an inexperienced man put in over his head. To add insult to injury, this was done with the connivance of his supposed Liberal friends, who were apparently willing to sacrifice one of their own for the sake of acquiring a small piece of bargaining power with the new government.

Now [Achille] is content to look upon his present position as a resting place, for with this precedent established by his friends there would be no hope of ever being promoted by the Conservatives. Our present plan is to give up housekeeping in the spring and board as cheaply as we decently can, for the next two or three years. During that time he will study French and Latin and work away at his drawing, going every vacation to Toronto to take lessons there, and as soon as he feels himself competent, to move to the States and try to be connected with some school or college, also to make what he can as a crayon artist.[6]

In spite of the discouragement of Achille's failure to win promotion, however, the Fréchettes did not leave Ottawa, but in fact settled into what was in many ways the happiest and most productive period of their lives. On the whole, they shared in the growing prosperity, consolidation of wealth and power, and relative contentment which the country enjoyed for the next seven or eight years. The period extending roughly from 1877 to 1885 saw an end to the economic recession of the 1870s, a huge increase in productivity and income in such agricultural staples as wheat, a significant rise in population through immigration and childbirth, a steady growth in the size and importance of Canadian cities, and perhaps most significant of all, this decade witnessed the completion of the great symbolic and practical expression of the hoped-for unification of Canada from sea to sea, the Canadian Pacific Railway.

The United States was experiencing even greater prosperity and growth in these years; but along with the accelerated industrialization, westward expansion, and urbanization came an atmosphere of materialism, cynicism, and corruption which Mark Twain was to label in disgust 'the Gilded Age.' Such things as political decadence, commercial dishonesty, and injustice were by no means excluded from Canada in this period, of course; but just as many activities and institutions in the northern country seemed somehow more leisurely and diminutive or less sinister than their counterparts in the United States, so the various manifestations of social and political vice seemed not so grossly evident in Canada. In the long run, Annie and Achille Fréchette probably congratulated themselves for ultimately deciding to remain in Ottawa.

Although he abandoned his ambitions to teach in the United States, Achille went ahead with his serious study of art. He had been an enthusiastic amateur in sketching and painting since childhood, but had never approached the activity in any systematic or academic fashion. Now, however, he enrolled in the small, newly established Ottawa School of Art, where, incidentally, he was for some time the only French-Canadian student, and where he studied with a talented young graduate of the Royal Canadian Academy, Montreal-born William Brymner. Subsequently, in 1882 and 1883, he studied painting and sketching briefly at the Art Students' League in New York City, where with William Dean Howells' patronage he met many distinguished American artistic and literary figures. In both years, however, his studies were interrupted, first by the death of his father in August 1882, and then by an unexpected revocation of his leave of absence from the translation office in the fall of 1883.

But in spite of this temporary failure to expand the arena of his artistic activities, he went on to distinguish himself locally in Ottawa, especially in portrait painting. He executed a series of portraits of distinguished Canadian political, literary, and social figures, including Mrs John G. Bourinot, Pamphile Le May, Octave Crémazie, and Louis-Joseph Papineau (the latter two presumably based on existing portraits and the memories of people who had known them in life). He also did some illustrations of fictional scenes and characters, one of which, entitled 'Pauvre Elise,' was based on a short story by his wife. And in 1883 Achille took no less than four prizes in a local competition held by the Ottawa Art Association, of which he was shortly thereafter elected to the executive.[7]

With all this newly stimulated artistic activity, and with the press of his professional duties, Achille found little time for his other avocation of literature. But even if he had had the time to write for publication, invidious members of the new Conservative government were continually on the watch for any public expressions of partisan feeling by civil servants, in defiance of the rules of their employment. As a known Liberal sympathizer, Achille was much safer expressing himself in visual rather than verbal art. Even so, Annie was reporting to her family early in 1881 that 'that nasty Tassé [journalist and Conservative MP Joseph Tassé] haunts Achille and threatens him on the grounds that he writes political articles for *La Patrie* of Montreal. Achille says he could swear that he has never written a political article since he went into office, but with this government one has not much chance.'[8] An unexpected recognition of Achille's literary achievements came in 1881 when his early poem 'Les Martyrs de la Foi au Canada' was chosen for inclusion in a new anthology of *La Poésie française au Canada*, edited by Louis H. Taché. But on the whole, throughout the 1880s, Achille was content to leave the literary activity for the family in the hands of his wife.

After her marriage, Annie gave up most of her regular newspaper correspondence, only continuing with the *New York Tribune*, and concentrating her literary efforts on magazine fiction. In March 1878 the *Youth's Companion* of Boston accepted a children's story from her entitled 'Poor Little Bobby,' which was her first work of fiction published under her married name. She also continued to place stories and articles with *Harper's* magazine. 'How That Cup Slipped' (September 1879) is a love story in the manner of her earlier 'Fireworks,' in which a promising romance comes to grief as a result of accidental circumstance. The treatment of this formula in 'How That Cup Slipped' includes a careful attention to details of character and setting, although there is some coyness in the tone, as when the narrator addresses a series of rhetorical questions to the sly suitors of her beautiful heroine. On the whole, however, the story is a reasonably good exploitation of the theme of unsuccessful love, a theme on which the *Harper's* editors had apparently changed their minds since their critique of Annie's earlier 'Visit to a Country House.'

'How That Cup Slipped' was not quite so dramatically effective, however, as Annie's next *Harper's* story, 'The Chances of War, and How One Was Missed' (September 1881), in which she almost succeeds in endowing the theme of unsuccessful love with tragic overtones. Here, the setting is somewhere in the South during the Civil War, and the lovers are a wounded Union officer and a Southern belle who takes him into her house to treat his wounds. The characters and situation could be easily sentimentalized, but Annie avoids triteness by endowing the narrative with a retrospective dream-like atmosphere, as her soldier hero recalls the experience many years after the war. The theme thus becomes the soldier's nostalgic obsession with what is now nothing more than a fragment of memory fading into an impersonal stereo-type, yet which still retains the power to dominate his life:

Now and then he would meet a bright, lovable girl who seemed not averse to win her way into his heart, and he would be half ready to admit her. But at the boundary line of that woman's kingdom a dream-maiden stood and waved back the intruder, and when he felt inclined to quarrel with her arrogant dominion, the dark eyes which met his accusations with conscious power smilingly lured him back to the past, and the shadowy hand which put away a rival was lifted tenderly to his lips to receive once more that farewell kiss, now grown into a pledge of constancy.[9]

Annie also produced a story with a Canadian setting, a realistic tale concerning the economic and romantic tribulations of a French-Canadian sewing girl in Quebec City. The tale was not acceptable, however, to the major American magazines which had taken her work in the past, and she finally had to settle for publication in a small New York weekly, *Our Continent*, edited by Albion Tourgée, an Ohio-born novelist whose French ancestry perhaps made him hospitable to fiction with French-Canadian setting and characters. '"Pauvre Elise" has at last found a home upon "Our Continent,"' Annie sardonically wrote her father and sisters, 'remuneration, $20.00.' Her brother William expressed his admiration for the 'simple unaffected reality' of the story: 'It is pitched in exactly the right key, and there is not a false note in it.'[10] But for some undiscernible reason, American editors seemed reluctant to publish fiction about Canada, even though they were quite willing to take Canadian subject matter in other forms, such as Annie's earlier travel articles on Quebec.

Whatever the explanation, 'Pauvre Elise' languished obscurely in the pages of *Our Continent* (and in the *Ashtabula Sentinel*, where it was copied by the editor, Annie's brother Joe), even though Annie had only recently scored one of her most notable literary successes with an article on a Canadian topic in *Harper's* magazine. In November 1878, the Marquis of Lorne had arrived in Canada with his wife Princess Louise, daughter of Queen Victoria, to take up his duties as governor-general. A British princess in North America was of great interest not only to Canadians but also to the people of the United States, who as Annie well knew were inveterate and awed observers of European royalty, in spite of their republican political ideals. Annie covered the arrival of the couple and their first public receptions for the *New York Tribune*, then set to work on a feature magazine article about them.

Princess Louise tended to be rather conscious of her regal dignity; as one historian says, 'Canadian society she found odious, and Canadians unpleasantly forward.'[11] So a personal interview, especially by an exuberant American unaccustomed to the fine points of court etiquette, seemed out of the question. But as the wife of a civil servant, Annie could get into the public levees and receptions which were part of the governor-general's obligations, and at least take careful note of the viceregal couple and their residence. The result of such observations was 'Life at Rideau Hall,' published in *Harper's*, July 1881, a detailed report on the elegant social life centred in the governor-general's mansion, as well as an appreciative account of the cultural contributions of the Marquis and Marchioness to Canada. In general, the article was the sort of description of remote 'high life' which was one characteristic type of popular feature in nineteenth-century American magazines; but its careful research and balanced reporting suggest once again that Annie's real literary strengths were in expository prose rather than in fiction. These strengths were illustrated again in another article for *Harper's*, 'Summer Resorts on the St. Lawrence' (July 1884), describing the popular steamer excursion from Quebec City to the Saguenay, and the magnificent scenery and picturesque tourist attractions along the route.

In 1883, Annie calculated that since 1868, when her first short story was published in a national magazine, she had earned roughly twenty-three hundred dollars from her magazine and newspaper contributions, which was a fairly respectable income over fifteen years for a part-time writer, and which suggests that if she had stayed with full-time authorship she might have been economically successful at least.[12] The leading American magazines like *Harper's* paid extremely well throughout the nineteenth century: 'Life at Rideau Hall' and 'Summer Resorts in the St. Lawrence,' for instance, had each earned one hundred and fifty dollars. The small and often short-lived contemporary magazines of English Canada, by contrast, were often unable to pay their contributors anything at all, a situation which explains why after gaining entry into *Harper's* and *Scribner's* and other prominent magazines, Annie wrote only very occasionally for Canadian publication. In this practice, she was not different from many native-born and presumably more nationalistic Canadian authors of the time, most of whom associated literary success with exposure in the front-ranking American periodicals.

But although her writing provided an attractive supplementary income and gained her a minor reputation as a feature journalist, Annie was mainly occupied with non-literary pursuits in the early years of her married life. In April 1878, her first child was born. The baby girl was named Marie-Marguérite, after a sister of Achille's who died in infancy, but very soon acquired the pet name 'Vevie,' by which she was known in the family for the rest of her life. In August 1879 the Fréchettes' second and last child was born, a son, who was given the name Howells.

This increase in their family inspired Annie and Achille to look for something larger than their current rented accommodation, and in the spring of 1881 they bought a house on MacKay Street in New Edinburgh, a village to the east of the city, on the Ottawa River. New Edinburgh was originally an industrial settlement, the site of a grist mill and sawmill built in the early nineteenth century by pioneer entrepreneur Thomas McKay, but by the time of the Fréchettes' removal it was a fairly exclusive residential suburb. Rideau Hall, which had originally been McKay's mansion, was situated there. Many members of Parliament and civil servants lived in New Edinburgh; the Fréchettes' neighbours were House of Commons Clerk and author John G. Bourinot and his wife. 'We are beginning to feel a little settled, and are greatly delighted with our house,' Annie wrote her brother Will in May; 'It is by far the most home-like place we have yet been in, and I think we are going to like the little village itself.'[13]

The comparative prosperity and contentment of the Fréchettes of Ottawa in the 1870s and 1880s were largely shared by their American and their Canadian relatives. Early in 1881, William Dean Howells finally made the decisive move of resigning from the editorship of the *Atlantic* to devote himself to the full-time writing of fiction. The increased time at his disposal enabled him to concentrate all his energies on a work more sociologically and psychologically profound than any he had ever attempted, his fictional anatomy of the disintegration of a marriage, *A Modern Instance* (1882). Besides producing many minor novels and short plays in the early 1880s, Howells climaxed this stage of his career with the work which to many readers was his best, and has certainly proved to be his most durable, the innovative study of an American businessman, *The Rise of Silas Lapham* (1885). With the latter novel, Howells became perhaps the best known, most influential, and one of the most prosperous authors in America.

There were, however, dark aspects to his success and prosperity: his daughter Winifred was showing increasing signs of a mysterious illness which was to prove fatal within a few years, and Howells himself suffered a severe physical collapse from overwork. Nevertheless, he managed in spite of illness and an enormous schedule of literary commitments to continue to indulge his lifelong passion for travel, and in the summer of 1882 he and his family made a brief visit to Canada. The Howellses were unable to make a convenient stopover in Ottawa, but they arranged to meet the Fréchettes in Montreal. Accompanied by little Vevie, who had been visiting her grandfather Howells, William and his family arrived by steamer in Montreal, where besides enjoying a pleasant visit with Annie and Achille, they watched an enthusiastic reunion between the children. 'The two funny little things,' he wrote his sister Victoria, 'took each other round the neck in an affecting and dramatic embrace ... Annie I found just as delightful as ever – there never was a more charming person.'[14]

On the other side of the family, Achille's brother Louis was also enjoying an abundance of professional success. His defeat in the election of 1878 led to a decision to pursue a full-time career in literature instead of returning to journalism, and in 1879 he published a new volume of poetry, *Les Fleurs boréales et Les Oiseaux de Neige*. Although still writing in the derivative idiom of the French romantics, Louis Fréchette achieved considerable popular and critical success by his use of distinctive North American settings and themes, as for instance in his famous narrative poem 'La Découverte du Mississippi.' In June 1880 he had two dramas on Canadian subjects produced in Montreal, *Le Retour de l'Exilé* and *Papineau*. And in the same month, to make his success complete, he learned that his recent volume of poetry had been awarded the prix Montyon by the Académie française. Later that summer, Louis made the first visit of his life to his beloved France to collect his 2000 franc prize, where his joy was consummated by a meeting with one of his most revered literary idols, Victor Hugo. The first Canadian author to be distinguished by the French Academy, Fréchette was thereafter known popularly to his compatriots as 'le

lauréat.' 'I rejoice most heartily in your success,' his sister-in-law Annie
wrote soon after the prix Montyon was announced, 'and feel sure it is
well earned'; though she went on to confess candidly, 'my faith in you
as a poet is quite blind, since I fear I can never really understand
French poetry, but Achille believes in you – and so, naturally, I do.'[15]

One further literary success was scored by the Fréchette family in
these halcyon years. Like William Dean Howells and almost everyone
at the Howells-Fréchette wedding, Annie had been fascinated by the
stories of Achille's brother Edmond about true adventure in the Canadian northwest, and she became convinced that Edmond could easily
make literary capital of these adventures. Accordingly, she wrote to the
Youth's Companion in 1878, shortly after that periodical had accepted
her story 'Poor Little Bobby,' to recommend Edmond as a prospective
author of stories or articles on the northwest frontier. The editors
returned a favourable reply, and contacted Edmond, who wrote to
Annie in June 1878: 'Messrs. Perry Mason & Co. [publishers of the
Youth's Companion], to whom you have spoken of me it appears as a
remarkable adventurer have written to me, and I am decided to try my
hand. I will send them something. I cannot guarantee though that it
will be masterpieces that they will get from this Frenchman.'[16]

The result, if not a masterpiece, was a series of highly readable
narrative and expository prose pieces published in 1879, on such
subjects as an overland march to Fort Walsh, the evils of the whisky
trade among the Indians of the Canadian prairies, the Sioux refugees
and renegades in Canada, a character sketch of Sitting Bull while he
was in the custody of a Mounted Police contingent which included
Edmond Fréchette, and various brief prose sketches of life in the
settlements and forts on the frontier. Annie was very much to be
commended for her literary encouragement of Edmond, but in a way it
was unfortunate that she directed him to the *Youth's Companion*, since
his stories and articles are by no means mere tales of adventure for
children but comparatively sophisticated and historically valuable
eyewitness records of the early Canadian West.[17]

Another important member of the Howells-Fréchette network of
relatives, William Cooper Howells, was also enjoying relative prosperity and contentment in the late 1870s and early 1880s. When President
Rutherford B. Hayes took office in 1877, Howells looked for the
possibility of a more lucrative consular appointment, especially with
the recommendation of his son, who had written Hayes's campaign
biography. The elder Howells and his daughters had been reasonably
happy in picturesque and socially intimate Quebec, but the income

from the consulship was simply not enough to give the family a decent living. Late in 1876 Victoria Howells wrote her brother Will a pitiful account of the family's straitened circumstances: 'Father's income barely keeps us. It doesn't allow us one luxury. Annie's earnings has clothed us three girls almost entirely since we came to Quebec, and getting her what she will have to have, and then losing what she has given us heretofore, will leave us that much worse off. Everything we have is wearing out, furniture, carpets, and all, and we dare not replace them.'[18] As events developed, William Cooper's reputation with the Hayes administration was strong enough not to need his son's recommendation; there was some talk of giving him the consular post at Montreal, but finally in April 1878 he was assigned to Toronto.

'The Canadians like father,' Annie wrote to her brother before William Cooper moved to Toronto, 'who has really made himself known in the best circles in Canada.'[19] For the next two years, Consul Howells continued to win the admiration of the Canadians and the approval of his superiors by discharging his duties with congenial efficiency. In 1880, however, the us presidential election inexorably rolled around, and like all political appointees, William Cooper found himself nervously awaiting the outcome. For the Americans in Toronto the suspense was particularly acute, because the margin of popular votes was the narrowest of any presidential election up to that time, and at first conflicting reports of the outcome came in over the telegraph. But finally the news came of the victory of the Republican candidate, James Garfield, an Ohio native and long-standing friend of the Howells family.

The life of the Garfield administration was to be lamentably short, however: the President was shot by a disappointed office seeker in July 1881, and died in September. His successor, Chester Arthur, was a stranger to William Cooper Howells, and was reported to be considering many changes in political appointments. The consul at Toronto feared for his position, but his security was restored by the intervention of personages no less prominent than Mark Twain and Ulysses Grant. William Dean Howells related the story in *My Mark Twain* (1910):

When my father was consul at Toronto during Arthur's administration, he fancied that his place was in danger, and he appealed to me. In turn I appealed to Clemens, bethinking myself of his friendship with Grant and Grant's friendship with Arthur. I asked him to write to Grant in my father's behalf, but No, he answered me, I must come to Hartford, and we would go on to New York together and see Grant personally ... We went to find Grant in his business office ... He was very simple and very cordial, and I was instantly the more at home with him, because his voice was the soft, rounded, Ohio River accent to which my years were earliest used ... When I stated my business he merely said, Oh no; that must not be; he would write to Mr. Arthur; and he did so that day; and my father lived to lay down his office, when he tired of it, with no urgence from above.[20]

William Cooper Howells tired of the consular service in 1883, and at the age of seventy-six retired to a farm in Virginia. His experiment with farming at such an advanced age and while in declining health was not a success; in a few years he was compelled to give it up and remove to the old family home at Jefferson. The southern sojourn lasted long enough, however, for him to entertain his Fréchette relatives from Canada during three summers, and for Annie to derive from her visits to Virginia some valuable literary inspiration.

Thus, as the 1890s approached, the Fréchettes found very little cause for discouragement, either in their own lives or in their observation of the lives of those closest to them. There were, inevitably, the usual day-to-day sources of irritation, temporary crises of illness or of professional disappointment or perhaps of social conflict. But the general spectacle of their lives in early middle age, viewed from the remote and selective perspective of the biographer, presents an outline of smooth and steady progress towards a degree of professional achievement and personal satisfaction such as few people can hope to experience. Annie was clearly not to be an author of her brother's stature, but she was happy in her domestic situation and gratified by her occasional modest successes in part-time journalism and fiction writing. Achille was committed to his civil-service routine, but he had plenty of leisure to indulge his artistic inclinations in painting and in the writing of an occasional poem. His professional functions, further-more, were not quite so dull and unromantic as they might appear to an uninformed observer. The routine of translation can, of course, be exciting to anyone who like Achille Fréchette is genuinely fascinated by the idiosyncrasies of language. But in more specific and more excep-tional terms, Achille's work in translation, combined with his lifelong interest in education, was shortly to precipitate him into a local public controversy in Ottawa, which in some ways was the most noteworthy event of his long professional career.

CHAPTER SEVEN

Achille Fréchette:
The Separate School Debate

Achille's professional situation under the Conservative government in the 1880s continued to involve some hostility directed against him as a known Liberal supporter. For a while this hostility was sorely aggravated, then was suddenly cleared up so that Achille was not only freed from his professional insecurity but was enabled to find a limited outlet for his strong political feelings. In the summer of 1882, Louis Fréchette had lost a bid to regain a seat in the Dominion Parliament, and all through that year and the next he made intermittent attacks against the Conservative government in the Montreal press. These attacks especially provoked the ire of Sir Hector Langevin, minister of public works and leader of the French-Canadian bloc in the Conservative party, and Langevin struck back indirectly by impeding Achille's chances for promotion. Achille remonstrated with Louis, but his attempts at restraining the poet's enthusiasm merely produced a temporary estrangement between the two brothers.

In desperation, Annie thought of appealing to her father, whose many prominent Canadian friends included Langevin. 'A letter from you to Langevin would do us more good than anything else,' Annie wrote her father. 'We thought if you would write him on the strength of your friendly acquaintance in Quebec, that what you would tell him would have all the more weight coming from a non-political source.'[1] William Cooper Howells was only too happy to oblige, not only out of natural regard for his daughter and son-in-law, but also undoubtedly because a similar service had recently been performed on his own behalf by Mark Twain and former president Grant. The requested letter reassuring Langevin of Achille's non-involvement in Louis' political activities was immediately forthcoming, and within a month Achille was not only reconciled to Langevin but had received a raise in salary. 'Your letter did it,' he wrote his father-in-law, 'and allow me to give you my most grateful thanks.'[2]

Canadian civil servants were supposed to be barred from overt political activity, but there was some official uncertainty about the application of this restriction to municipal politics. In 1888, encouraged by his generally favourable standing with the government, Achille stood for election to the Ottawa separate school board; to his gratification his success went unchallenged by his superiors in the civil service. Technically, Achille was neither a Catholic nor a separate school supporter; he had virtually abandoned his religion under the early influence of his brother Louis and the rationalistic republican sentiments which prevailed among French-Canadian intellectuals in the United States when Achille was in Chicago. He had officially left the church at the time of his marriage, and his two children attended public school in Ottawa. But the separate school board of bilingual Ottawa was divided into French and English sections, and Achille was particularly interested in the status of French-language instruction. Over the years, he had become more and more convinced of the validity of the principle suggested to him by the teaching brothers at the Collège de Lévis, that English was the language of Canadian business and politics while French was to be preserved and cultivated as the expression of the distinctive French-Canadian identity, and especially as the medium of literature. Of the acceptable academic standards of the anglophone schools he had little doubt; but in the schools where French was the predominant language of instruction, the standards were reputed to be decidedly inferior. Hence Achille felt that his services could be best put to use in the French division of the separate school board.

French-language instruction in English Canada, along with the frequently related problem of the role of the Catholic church in education, had been vexed questions since the earliest days of settlement in Upper Canada, when French-speaking immigrants from the lower province had begun to move westward almost simultaneously with the arrival of English-speaking settlers from the United States and Great Britain. In eastern Ontario, and especially in Ottawa, the problem was particularly acute by the 1880s, when at least one-third of the region's population were French-speaking Catholics. Entire townships and sections of the city were virtually unilingually French, as were many of the 'bilingual' schools which had been created by provincial legislation in an attempt to achieve a compromise between the establishment of

English as the official language of the province and the recognition of the aspirations of minorities to maintain contact with their ancestral cultures. The bilingual schools in Ontario were entitled to either public or separate status, according to local preference, although in practice most bilingual schools were French and Catholic, since the available teachers were almost all clerics recruited from Quebec. In Ottawa, the city's separate school board had several bilingual schools under its jurisdiction, in which most of the teaching was done by French-speaking Roman Catholic priests, nuns, and brothers. In 1886 the board had recognized the de facto French status of these schools by dividing itself into French and English sections and giving the French section authority over the bilingual schools.[3]

Very soon after his election Achille found himself centrally involved in a controversy over the academic standards and administrative procedures of the bilingual separate schools in Ottawa. On 18 September 1888, according to a contemporary account in the *Ottawa Citizen*, a member of the French section of the board named G. Marsan brought forth a list of complaints against certain francophone 'Christian Brothers' (members of the Frères des Écoles chrétiennes order) teaching in various Ottawa bilingual separate schools. The Brothers allegedly exceeded their authority in matters of discipline, and used a distinctly coercive brand of spiritual instruction while neglecting academic subjects. 'If a boy was late for church,' Marsan charged, 'he lost all his good marks for the week ... Boys and girls who were unable to subscribe to funds for presents for priests and others on the occasion of their fête days lost their marks as punishment. The Christian Brothers, in a word, did not care a snap for the trustees, and did just as they pleased.' 'Mr. Fréchette,' the *Citizen* went on to report, 'asked if these teachers could be made to recognize the board at all.'[4]

The local Catholic authorities were predictably quick to respond, although at first their response was not made in public, nor was it particularly effective or even intelligent. A local inspector of bilingual separate schools, M.L. Dauray, was present at the meeting on the 18th, and had made no particular comment on the charges of Marsan and Fréchette; but somehow Dauray's parish priest Father Gonthier got the idea that the inspector supported their opinions, and sent Dauray a letter of rebuke, concluding with the picayune announcement that henceforth the parish would no longer require Dauray's services as organist in St-Jean Baptiste Church. Within a few weeks this ill-conceived letter found its way into the columns of *Le Canada*, at that time a moderate French Catholic newspaper of uncommitted politics.

Annoyed by this underhanded and clumsy persecution of an inno-
cent party, Achille made a vehement public attack on Gonthier – an
attack which was obviously calculated to be doubly insulting by being
delivered in English, in an anglophone newspaper. 'The Fat in the
Fire,' the *Citizen* gleefully proclaimed on 18 October, by way of intro-
ducing a two-part letter addressed to Gonthier by Fréchette, in which
he rebuked his opponent for the cowardly attack on Dauray and went
on to expose the illogicality or falsehood of virtually every statement in
Gonthier's letter to the inspector. Gonthier had charged that 'pretenti-
ous nonentities' occupied a certain number of seats on the board;
Fréchette pointed out that Gonthier himself had actively supported
from the pulpit all the current francophone members of the board.
Gonthier had claimed that the board should concern itself exclusively
with business matters such as salary negotiation and building mainte-
nance, and leave academic matters entirely to the teachers; Fréchette
replied that 'the board hires and pays its teachers, and insists ... that as
employer it has the right to see that services paid for are faithfully and
honestly done.' Furthermore, Achille argued,

while the board are in all circumstances willing to show, and do show, the
greatest courtesy and deference to the religious dignitaries in connection with
the schools, yet we are in these matters accountable to the electors, and not in
the slightest degree amenable to you, reverend father, as a priest ... Without
fear of condemnation from the highest tribunals of the church, I point out [*sic*]
to the electors or parents as being the primary authorities in these matters, and
we as their representatives are delegated their responsibilities ... If a layman,
reverend father, may be allowed to address you on such matters, I will ask you
if it is not the doctrine of the church that in education the primary right
belongs to the parents, and that the church claims right of interference only on
their absence, or when they neglect the exercise of their natural right ... This is
the doctrine of the church, not one of my making. St. Thomas Aquinas, the
greatest light of your Order, gave it its embodiment in the following words: '...
We receive from our parents, being, food, and education ... Of these three
things the principal is the last, for it touches most closely the end proposed by
nature.' If your stand, reverend father, is not in conformity with this doctrine, I
respectfully submit that either the doctrine or your position must be wrong.[5]

This, as far as Gonthier and the church were concerned, was an
infuriating challenge. Not only was the devil quoting scripture – or at
least he was quoting Aquinas – but he was doing so in the heretical
language of English. More basically, however, Fréchette was placing

the whole quarrel in the larger context of the question of secular versus ecclesiastical authority, a question which had plagued Canadian politics since the earliest days of the old French régime. This controversy, furthermore, had ramifications which extended in various directions and involved several kinds of political, religious, and ethnic conflict. As an internecine French-Canadian quarrel, Fréchette's attack on church authority over education raised the continuing issue of ultramontane versus liberal Catholics: that is, the conflict between those who looked to Rome for the ultimate judgment on all questions, including questions of national or local politics, and those who defended the responsibility of secular authority in all questions not obviously involving religion.

In partisan political terms, the controversy could also be seen in relation to the opposition between Liberal and Conservative, since ultramontane Catholics tended to gravitate towards Conservatism as a lesser evil while French-Canadian Liberals advocated the secularization of Canadian society and increased rapport between French and English. In Ottawa, a city which was ethnically almost a microcosm of the nation, the quarrel also encompassed the rivalry between French and English, a ramification which Fréchette deliberately invoked by publishing his attack in an English newspaper, thus inviting English support for his side of the controversy.

The ultramontanes lost no time in launching their counter-attack. Nor did they leave their defence to a feeble spokesman like Father Gonthier. Battle was joined by an author signing himself 'Raphael,' whose identity was never declared publicly, but who was obviously an experienced and fluent ultramontane polemicist. As might be expected, Raphael did not meet the enemy on his own ground of the anglophone *Citizen*, because to do so would have been to admit an important premise of Fréchette's argument, namely that the controversy was the business of the whole community and not exclusively of the francophone population. Withdrawing to the columns of *Le Canada*, Raphael launched a withering – and protracted – denunciation of Fréchette and his allies and their ideas. The nineteenth century was the great age of public debates, of letters to the editor and pamphlet wars, and French-Canadian writers were undoubtedly among those who helped raise this activity to the status of an art. Unfortunately for the ultramontane cause, however, Raphael had obviously mastered every principle of the art except brevity. For twelve interminable instalments he attacked the enemy's position, point by trivial point, until his readers must have agreed with Achille's suggestion in his subsequent brief reply that the editor would sigh with relief for the liberation of his subscribers.

Raphael's argument, stripped of its repetitions, synopses, and rhetorical flourishes, turned on two main points. First, Fréchette's accusations were unworthy of consideration because they were made in a 'journal anglais et protestant'; second, all the accusations against the teaching Frères could be categorically denied, except the accusation that they forced children to attend school on Sunday for religious instruction: this, Raphael insists, the teaching clerics have every right to do. This second point involved the essence of the ultramontane position: the church has a right to demand attendance and obedience of its adherents and their children. Indeed, when the subject is brought to this kind of ultimate challenge, the church has the right to control in all matters, both temporal and spiritual, all segments of the Catholic population – including, the writer adds darkly, the school board. The series ends, appropriately, with a recommendation that the school board be reorganized to ensure that the French section is staffed by true Catholics.[6]

Throughout the Raphael articles there are frequent appeals to the sense of French-Canadian Catholic identity which must at all costs avoid contamination from English Protestant ideas. There are also repeated implicit and explicit declarations of the supremacy of the church, a supremacy which, as his concluding instalment makes clear, does not stop with purely moral or spiritual matters, but can be legitimately extended to all aspects of Catholic life. In the course of this argument, liberal democratic social philosophy is inevitably swept aside: the fact that the school board is created by popular election, for instance, is dismissed as an unfortunate practice which would be better replaced by a system of selection designed to guarantee the religious orthodoxy of the members. In effect, Raphael as an extreme ultramontanist advocates an ecclesiastical oligarchy in which the church would be given complete control over its adherents.

Fréchette's brief one-instalment reply, published in *Le Canada* on 19 November, did not waste time on a point-by-point review of what was after all an interminable argument based on radically opposed philosophies. Instead, he called attention to Raphael's contemptible techniques of argumentation, such as the gratuitous bitterness of his tone, the pettiness of his charges (he had implied at one point that his opponents must have been drunk when they dared criticize the Frères), his frequent and unsupported innuendo against individuals, and especially his cowardly refuge in a pseudonym, 'ce bouclier des lâches, ce masque des voleurs de réputations.'

The main point of Fréchette's reply, however, arose out of an accusation Raphael had made indirectly and in passing in an early article. Because Fréchette had quoted Aquinas in one of his *Citizen* letters, Raphael implied that he must have had some help from a scholar of the University of Ottawa, since such an obviously unintellectual heretic could hardly be expected to have first-hand knowledge of theology. Raphael thus clumsily revealed an obvious sore point within the church, namely a tension between the ultramontane parochial priesthood and the more liberal ecclesiastics of the university. Achille did not bother pointing out this dissension, however, but stuck to the main point of reassuring the public that he did indeed have some knowledge of Aquinas, and this slur against the university theologians was merely another of Raphael's cowardly character assassinations: 'j'ai autre chose à faire que suivre sur son terrain le premier Basile venu qui pieusement se gaudit de pouvoir ainsi faire le mal *incognito*. Ces saints écorcheurs du prochain s'inquiètent bien que leur victime soit trouvée demain éventrée à Whitechapel, pourvu que leur dessein soit accompli et que leur masque ait sauvé leur nuque des mains de la police.'[7] As far as the theological controversy was concerned, it could, Fréchette stated, be reduced to the conclusive biblical text 'render unto Caesar'; and no competent theologian, he insisted, would profane these words of the Evangelist.

Raphael's reply was equally brief, and predictable. In *Le Canada* of 25 November he rejected *in toto* Fréchette's argument, insisted that public sympathy would be on the side of those who defended the church rather than those who attacked it, and, without deigning to discuss the issue of his anonymity, concluded by suggesting that Fréchette was more to be pitied than censured. Since this reply offered no new arguments, it called for no rebuttal, and Achille did not make any. The controversy was thus fought to a standstill in the press, with no resultant action on the complaints against allegedly incompetent teachers in the bilingual separate schools, and there for the time being the matter rested.

The following year Achille was elected chairman of the French committee of the separate school board. His tenure, however, was to be extremely brief. He was soon engaged in another public controversy, again initiated in the anglophone press, and still involving the question of church authority over education. The point at issue was an attempt by the Archbishop of Ottawa to introduce a teaching order of nuns into one of the local schools without the board's approval; but Achille's public statement on the matter was primarily concerned with the larger question of whether the church or the board was to have control of

French Catholic education. In an open letter to the Archbishop in the *Evening Journal* of 21 December 1889, Fréchette grimly declared that the board 'could not in honesty and self-respect serve as a screen, or hold the trust vested in us by the civil law for the benefit of an order of things not contemplated by it; we could not be mere instruments for the legalization of a will substituted to that recognized in the statute.'[8] The Archbishop was adamant in his decision, and refused even to discuss the matter publicly, other than to invoke the supremacy of church authority over all Catholics, and Fréchette and his supporters had no recourse but to resign en masse in protest.

This abrupt end to Achille's official connection with the Ottawa separate school board did not, however, mark the end of his active involvement in questions relating to French Catholic education. In 1893 a local Irish priest named Whelan, in the course of a public castigation in the *Journal* of a university professor who had allegedly usurped ecclesiastical authority, made a passing comparative reference to 'the wretched anti-Episcopal campaign of falsehood and abuse conducted by the members of the French committee' of the school board four years previously. Fréchette was immediately in print with a retort, again maintaining that officials 'elected to an office under the law by the people' should be strictly free from any kind of ecclesiastical or other interest.[9] Once again the vital point at issue as far as Achille was concerned was the conflict between a liberal democratic social philosophy and an oligarchy which not only imposed its authority arbitrarily but also contributed to the deterioration of society by fostering a reactionary and academically inferior educational system. Whelan declined to enter into public debate, only suggesting in print that certain people should mind their own business, so Achille had to be content with replying briefly in kind, adding that 'if my commonplace choice of words is not equal to the occasion, I must offer the excuse that I was not, nor were my ancestors, born under the shadow of Blarney castle.'[10]

This latest exchange of public insults subsided fairly quickly, but in the larger context of provincial and national politics the related questions of separate schools and French-language education were obviously coming to a head. By 1893, a furious legal battle was raging in Manitoba as a result of anglophone attempts to eliminate publicly supported francophone schools in that province, and this battle was to become a key issue in the Dominion election of 1896. Throughout these years problems relating to bilingual and separate schools were a continuing source of political and social tension in Ontario, and in the

spring of 1895 a public quarrel broke out in the Ottawa press once
again.

It is difficult to tell from the strongly partisan contemporary newspaper accounts who started the new squabble; undoubtedly both sides
shared the blame. Certain anglophone and liberal elements on the
separate school board, apparently inspired by the partial success of the
Manitoba government, began a movement to secularize the local
schools, specifically by getting rid of the teaching order of the Frères
des Ecoles chrétiennes. The Frères had recently been demanding
substantial salary increases, and when the board refused their demands the Frères had unwisely taken to the newspapers to raise a cry of
'godless schools,' 'French revolution,' 'no respect for the clergy,' and so
forth. The board countered with accusations reminiscent of those
levied by Fréchette and Marsan seven years before. The Frères, said
the board, exploited their position by conducting a brisk and profitable
business forcing their pupils to buy textbooks of the Frères' own
devising, textbooks which were academically unacceptable. Of these
home-made books, the most outrageously bad were those purporting
to teach English composition and grammar.

An argument thus turning on the quality of language instruction as
well as ecclesiastical authority was bound to attract Achille Fréchette,
even though he had had no official connection with the board for some
time. Oddly enough, considering that one prominent bone of contention was the quality of English instruction, the battle was fought entirely in the francophone press. The Frères and their supporters took
to the pages of *Le Canada*, which had been sold in 1894 and was now a
virulently conservative ultramontane Catholic mouthpiece. The critics
of the Frères responded in *Le Temps*, a newspaper edited by Oscar
McDonnell, an experienced and literate francophone journalist (in
spite of his Irish name) renowned for his support of liberal causes and
his frequent attacks on the church. The first volleys merely assassinated
characters and condemned vice; then on 26 March *Le Canada* reported
on an 'assemblée considérable' of former students of the Frères des
Ecoles chrétiennes, which approved a resolution repudiating the criticisms levied against their former teachers. The assembly further resolved 'que les anciens élèves ... reconnaissent au clergé le droit de con-
trôler l'enseignement dans ces écoles et de diriger les contribuables
dans tout ce qui peut promouvoir les intérêts de ces mêmes écoles.'[11]
Here again was the old contention between ecclesiastical and secular
authority in education. Achille Fréchette was in print the following day
with a reply, 'Nos Ecoles locales – finie la Comédie,' signing himself

'Un Père' in accordance with the preference of *Le Temps* for pseudonyms, although the author was promptly recognized by his *Le Canada* opponents.

Achille had received his own elementary education from the Frères des Ecoles chrétiennes, and had derived many of his most firmly held intellectual inclinations from them, a fact which he was more than ready to acknowledge. His assumption that English was the dominant language of business and politics in Canada while French was the vital medium for the preservation of French-Canadian culture, and his belief in the value of profession-oriented education: these were principles learned from the Frères at the Collège de Lévis. But he had been educated in another time, another place; the Ottawa Frères of 1895 were but pale imitations of the giants of his own childhood. 'L'Institut des frères des écoles chrétiennes a, sans conteste, et surtout a eu, a l'époque où la réputation des frères était à faire au Canada, des écoles ou l'enseignement était d'un ordre autrement plus élevé.'[12] Now, Achille suggested, the Frères in Ottawa were merely trying to ride on the past academic reputation of their order, a reputation to which many of their teaching members in this degenerate day were not entitled. Their inferiority to their predecessors could be easily seen in the linguistic abilities of their pupils, as for example in the quotations from the resolutions passed at the recent assembly of former pupils, published in *Le Canada*.

The article was not the best of Achille's contributions to the school controversy. He had lost his temper, and perhaps was weary of repeatedly going over the same ground. So instead of reasserting his liberal credo, he focused on the specific issue of the composition and grammar of his opponents. This theme could yield some scorching invective: the resolution of the assembly was 'un ragoût de phrases informes la plupart ni françaises ni anglaises, mais tout fortement mêlées d'iroquois, dans lesquelles les barbarismes et les plus monstrueuses fautes de grammaire, de construction et de style font au bon sens et à la logique une guerre absolument désastreuse.' But it was also an invitation to a nit-picking contest. As might have been expected, *Le Canada* attacked Fréchette's composition and grammar, in a series of no less than four articles threatening to surpass the earlier efforts of 'Raphael' in prolixity and dullness. Fréchette responded briefly in kind, *Le Canada* returned the fire, and after a few further exchanges reflecting on the opponents' respective writing abilities the latest stage in the Ottawa separate school controversy petered out.

In the summer of 1895 the Ontario provincial government established a commission to investigate the bilingual separate schools in Ottawa. Various factors led to the creation of the commission, the most obvious of which was the direct request for provincial government intervention expressed by the Ottawa separate school board itself, which had had to deal with repeated complaints about the academic standards of the bilingual schools under its jurisdiction. It is surely legitimate to infer, however, that the lastest newspaper debate also had an influence on the provincial government's intervention in the Ottawa situation. One of the results of the commission's findings was the expulsion of the Frères des Ecoles chrétiennes from the Ottawa separate school system, although they were back within a year. Thereafter the bilingual separate school question in Ottawa seems to have drifted along in relative quiet in spite of the failure to effect any significant changes in the situation, until 1910, when a virulent and protracted province-wide eruption of a debate over French-language and Catholic education finally led to new legislation. The legislation was, however, the source of new quarrels; and thus the whole question of French-language education in Ontario continued through a vehement and frequently bitter dialectic which even to the present day has eluded ultimate solution.

After 1895 Achille Fréchette took no further direct part in the Ottawa schools quarrels, being increasingly occupied with professional matters especially after the Liberal victory in the Dominion election of 1896. In the larger context of the continuing debates over parochial schools and French-language education in nineteenth-century Canada, the small and localized controversy in which he was engaged has been overshadowed by more flamboyant province- and nation-wide arguments. Nevertheless, the Ottawa controversy of 1888–95, besides offering a fascinating example of typical debating techniques in nineteenth-century Canadian journalism, constitutes an unobtrusive but distinguished illustration of Achille Fréchette's literary ingenuity and versatility.

CHAPTER EIGHT

Annie Howells Fréchette:
Further Literary Ventures

While Achille was occupied with his newspaper duels and his other professional and artistic pursuits, Annie continued with her own absorbing literary and personal activities. In the summer of 1883 she and her two children visited William Cooper Howells at the farm in Virginia to which he had recently retired; before setting out on her travels, she got in touch with her brother William and a few editors to see if there might be a market for descriptive articles based on the excursion. H.M. Alden of *Harper's* and R.W. Gilder of *Scribner's* were encouraging but non-committal, and William as usual urged her to try fiction rather than expository prose. 'Why not put your material in the form of a story, or the adventures of some supposed family going from the north to Virginia with a realistic account of what they missed and what they found there? I think you might do this very charmingly.'[1]

For once, William's advice based on his preference for fiction over journalism turned out to be well taken. The idyllic reunions with her father and sisters over four successive summers between 1883 and 1886 suggested at first the possibility of some sort of general literary tribute involving the family, and in the fall of 1886 she wrote William for advice: 'Most ever since our marriage I have written two letters a week, to either father or the girls. They have saved the letters and Achille gathered them up and brought them back with us. Of course they form a complete journal of our life, and now a clamorous public formed of Achille, father and the girls, think I might edit them, and make a book which might be called Our First Ten Years, or something of that sort.'[2] William's response was, as always, both critical and encouraging: 'I have been thinking over the question you asked me about your letters, and I doubt if you could edit them so as to escape identification with them. They would have to be copied, anyway, and why not eliminate the letter-character, which [is] always repugnant in literature, and make a little story of your life which should be chiefly a biography of your children, with an *entourage* of housekeeping? This would be amusing and popular, and I think very novel. Make the children the central idea.'³

The suggestion of a story focusing on her children, together with the lingering reminiscences of Virginia, worked on Annie's imagination. In February 1887, Howells wrote his father that 'I've had a letter from Annie enclosing a charming little sketch of your calf "Juno" which I've sent to the St. Nicholas for her.'⁴ *St. Nicholas* was a New York-based magazine which, under the editorship of Mary Mapes Dodge, was revitalizing children's literature in America by discouraging the traditional formulas of condescending morality and saccharine style, in favour of a sympathy and respect for the intellectual and imaginative capacities of young readers. Annie had produced children's stories before, but her previous efforts in this vein had been traditional concoctions of sentiment and ponderous morality. 'Juno,' however, brought to the medium of children's literature an application of the principles of realism which delighted both William Dean Howells and the *St. Nicholas* editors.

The story is a slight and casual anecdote, apparently taken directly from experience. Two children visiting their grandfather's farm in Virginia decide to rescue Juno the calf from the ignominy of having to wear a restraining device for cattle; they take the calf away to live with them, and are found a few hours later by the disconcerted but indulgent adults in a cabin on the edge of the woods. The story is told in the rather formal prose typical of nineteenth-century children's literature, but with no artificial or affected attempt to condescend to young readers. 'Juno' appeared in the November 1887 issue of *St. Nicholas*, and the editors were pleased enough with it to accept a sequel, another children-and-animals story about the little visitors' acquisition of a pup, 'Bingo Was His Name,' published in June 1889.

Over the next seven or eight years, Annie wrote five more stories about the children at their grandfather's farm in Virginia, all unpretentious vignettes in the manner of the first two, dealing with such ordinary events as the farm cat's new litter of kittens, an excursion with grandfather after a load of coal, overheard childish speculations about the existence of fairies, and so on. After having been so often reluctant to make fiction out of her own personal experience, Annie had obviously struck a new and delightful chord in writing about the experiences of her children. Encouraged by the favourable editorial response to her farm stories, she began to think of publishing a small collection of them in book form. William, who had no direct experience with children's literature, could offer no firsthand advice about publishers, but he suggested that Annie consult the editors of the *Youth's Companion*, who had previously published the work of both Annie and her protégé, Edmond Fréchette.

One of the editors of the *Youth's Companion* in 1896 was Edward William Thomson, an author like the Fréchettes with cultural and personal ties on both sides of the Canada-US border. Born near Toronto, Thomson had served briefly in both the Union army during the American Civil War and the Canadian militia during the Fenian raids of 1866; he had been an editorial writer for the Toronto *Globe* from 1878 to 1891, and he worked for the *Youth's Companion* in Boston between 1891 and 1901, after which he moved to Ottawa, where he inevitably took a prominent part in the local cultural scene which included the Fréchettes. In 1895, Thomson had published his *Old Man Savarin and Other Stories*, a volume of light and sentimental local colour fictional sketches of the French, Scottish, Irish, and other settlers of eastern Ontario. Although a writer in what can be labelled a 'popular' vein – his stock in trade consisted mainly of comic dialect, melodrama, and surprise endings – Thomson was not really a children's author, and his years with the *Youth's Companion* were apparently not entirely happy.

But professing himself delighted to be of assistance to the sister of William Dean Howells, Thomson agreed to help Annie find a book publisher for her stories. His knowledge of American publishing was neither extensive nor specialized, however, and he merely sent the stories to some of the more prominent firms, such as Copeland & Day and Estes & Lauriat, who inevitably declined on the grounds that they did not ordinarily handle juvenile literature. The 1890s were not particularly prosperous years for the American publishing industry, whose fortunes tended to be speculative and erratic at the best of times. A number of bankruptcies and take-overs reflected the unsettled conditions which were to climax in the disappearance of many small companies and the emergence, around the turn of the century, of the modern corporate giants of the business, such as Scribner's, Harper's, and Doubleday. Only the most knowledgeable observer could have interpreted the signs in 1896, however, and directed an author to a company which could be reliably expected to have at least the minimal resources necessary for a book's success. As it happened, Thomson finally sent Annie's manuscript to the American Baptist Publishing Society of Philadelphia, a company of somewhat grandiose pretensions which supplied books in large quantities to churches and schools. To the author's delight, the Baptists accepted her stories, and Annie joyfully awaited their appearance.

To their credit, the Philadelphia company did an excellent job of production. Dividing the stories into two slim quarto volumes of about one hundred pages each, they provided a fine set of colour illustrations, a large clear text on glossy paper, and handsomely embossed stiff covers of light brown. *On Grandfather's Farm* and *The Farm's Little People* both appeared in the fall of 1897. William Dean Howells' response to the books, although obviously reflecting his emotional involvement with the subject, was a valid critical judgment: 'It is a perfect picture of child character and child thought ... charmingly simple and natural.'[5] Yet in spite of the undeniable charm of the stories and the attractiveness of the format, the books did not sell. Their matter-of-fact realism may have aroused the distaste of readers more accustomed to large doses of sentiment and melodrama, but Mary Mapes Dodge's *St. Nicholas* had trained a whole generation of children to accept the representation of the familiar and commonplace in literature, so Annie's judgment that the distributing methods of the publisher were at fault seems valid.

For the next ten years and more, correspondence passed back and forth between Annie and Philadelphia, in which the author tried to stir the publishers from their apparent lethargy and the publishers replied with explanations and excuses. There was brief cause for optimism when the George N. Morang publishing company of Toronto agreed tentatively to issue Canadian editions in consequence of the books being placed on a supplementary reading list for Ontario schools, but this deal did not materialize. Ultimately the American Baptist Publication Society issued only one edition, which appears to have languished in the few bookstores within its limited scheme of distribution.[6]

Fortunately, Annie continued to enjoy modest success in magazine and newspaper writing, to compensate for the disappointment with the children's books. In 1888 *Harper's Bazar* (thus the magazine's title was spelled until 1929) accepted a story from her entitled 'McDonald and Company, Builders,' about a contractor who is devastated by the death of his only son but is ultimately aroused from depression by his energetic daughter who takes the son's place and helps her father in the building of a house. This interesting plot motif of the self-assertive young female intruding on traditionally male professional territory (a reflection, perhaps, of the author's own early experiences in journalism) is awkwardly combined with a sentimental love story obviously tailored for the genteel *Bazar* reader. The female building contractor believes herself to be courted by a young man, but the supposed suitor turns out in the end to be attracted to the girl's demure and conventionally feminine younger sister.

This story of misunderstood romantic attentions, combined with a narrative about housebuilding, is a curious realignment of prominent elements in William Dean Howells' novel, *The Rise of Silas Lapham*, published just three years earlier. Annie was in all likelihood not consciously rewriting the love story of her brother's novel, but William could not help noticing the resemblance, to which he was probably referring with a touch of harmless irony when he wrote to praise his sister's story. 'It is a very neat bit of work, very simple and life-like, with some real heart-throbs in it. The girl going to see her father in the new house, that is a pretty scene; and the fellow falling in love with her sister instead of her is nice and new.'[7]

Annie also published in the *New England Magazine* of October 1890 a sentimental love story, 'Isabel, Elsie, and I,' again involving a young man who is presumed to be in love with one sister but actually turns out to be attracted to another. Encouraged by the initial success of her stories of grandfather's farm in *St. Nicholas*, she tried her hand at more writing for children, including 'A Jolly Lark: A Story for Boys' (in the *Chicago Standard*, and the *Toronto Daily Mail*, December 1890), 'Bill' (in *Wide Awake*, a children's annual, 1892), 'Donald's Will and Way' (in the *American Agriculturalist*, August 1894). These stories attempted to invoke the empathy with the thoughts and experiences of children which provided the essential charm of the tales of grandfather's farm, but the manufactured characters and situations lack interest, and the tone is generally that of the superior adult chuckling condescendingly over the foibles of young people.

Perhaps Annie's two most successful ventures in fiction during this period were 'How Cassie Saved the Spoons' and 'The Jones's Telephone,' published in *McClure's* magazine of September and October 1893, respectively. The first, about three young women and a child alone in a farmhouse who contrive to frighten off an intruding vagabond, probably reflects character elements of Annie and her sisters, as well as reminiscences of life in Jefferson. The second tale is a slight but interesting comic vignette reflecting the social impact of the advent of the telephone. 'Cassie' was subsequently chosen for reprinting in *Tales from McClure's: Adventure*, and the telephone story was included in *Tales from McClure's: Humor* (both 1897). In addition, Annie entered into a syndication arrangement with *McClure's*, whereby that magazine agreed to distribute those stories accepted for publication to various newspapers subscribing to its syndicate.

Although Annie directed most of her literary efforts to the more prominent American magazines, she was not entirely neglectful of Canadian publication. The fiction-writing sister of William Dean Howells enjoyed modest fame among the culturally knowledgeable segment of Ottawa's population, and in April 1895 she was invited by a local women's group to edit a special edition of the *Ottawa Journal*, to be written entirely by female contributors as a charity project in aid of the local free library. Annie's extensive newspaper experience was put to good use in attracting and organizing a collection of articles on the usual domestic topics and a few unusual topics, such as women's participation in politics and business. She herself contributed a short story, 'Love has a Conscience,' on the evils of drink, a timely subject since the agitation of the Women's Christian Temperance Union and other prohibitionist organizations was about to make liquor legislation a minor issue in the 1896 Dominion election, although Annie's tale contributed nothing but more emotion to the controversy. In 1896, an ambitious group of Ottawa literati attempted to start a cultural magazine entitled the *Lounger*, in emulation of the *Atlantic* and similar American periodicals, and Annie contributed a children's story entitled 'Jerry.' But the perennial situation in Canadian culture of local indifference and American competition prevailed in this instance, and the *Lounger* ceased publication in 1897 after a handful of issues.

Throughout their period of residence in Ottawa, both Annie and Achille Fréchette were prominent figures on the Ottawa cultural scene, taking active part in local activities and socializing with many prominent individuals, including the new generation of poets emerging in the 1880s and 1890s. It would be satisfying to know more about the Fréchettes' acquaintance, particularly with Archibald Lampman, Duncan Campbell Scott, and Wilfred Campbell, but relevant manuscript evidence is disappointingly small, since the individuals, all living in relative proximity to each other, had few occasions to exchange letters.

The extant evidence does reveal, however, several social relationships worth noting. In a letter to her sister Aurelia dated 12 February 1891, Annie described a recent cultural 'evening' held at her home, attended by several local writers and patrons of the arts. The proud maternal emphasis on a recitation by twelve-year-old Vevie is understandable in a family letter, but the Canadian literary historian cannot help yearning for more details concerning 'a poem' read that evening by 'Mr Archibald Lampman.'[8] Other evidence, however, indicates at least that the Fréchettes were on fairly cordial terms with Lampman and his wife. Among the Fréchette family papers is a note of Christmas greeting dated 1890, signed jointly by Lampman and Duncan Campbell Scott, and on the back is an autograph copy of Lampman's poem 'The Hermit Thrush.' In 1892, Annie wrote Aurelia about a recent 'little party' hosted by Achille and herself, and attended by 'two or three artists, some musical people, Archibald Lampman, Duncan Scott, and Wilfred Campbell, with their wives.'[9] But again, the letter is frustratingly short on detail, being devoted mainly to an anecdote about young Howells Fréchette.

Lampman's friendship with the Fréchettes is unfortunately most explicitly inferred from the circumstances immediately following the poet's death in 1899 at the lamentably early age of thirty-eight. Achille Fréchette arranged a local memorial tribute, upon which an Ottawa newspaper briefly reported:

On Saturday evening the last of a series of pleasant assemblies of literary people was given by Mrs. Fréchette, and it was one of the most interesting of those held. Mr. William Wilfred Campbell, at the close of the evening, read a poem in memory of the late Archibald Lampman, called 'The Bereavement of the Fields.' It seemed a very appropriate place in which to read the beautiful words of appreciation written by a brother poet – for on the Saturday preceding Lampman's death he was one of a brilliant trio of writers who met in Mrs. Fréchette's drawing room.[10]

One of the 'brilliant trio' and a regular member of the Fréchettes' cultural circle was Achille's fellow civil servant, Duncan Campbell Scott. In 1893, Scott presented Annie with an autograph copy of his poem, 'In November,' and Annie eventually responded to this and other of his works with the 'sincerest form of flattery.' Her brief fictional sketch, 'A Widow in the Wilderness,' published in *Harper's*, December 1899, and dealing with a pathetic confrontation between a taciturn Indian woman and a group of white men, obviously reflects Scott's poetic and prose vignettes of Indian life, gleaned from his field experience with the Department of Indian Affairs. Unfortunately, Annie lacked Scott's firsthand experience of the grim hardships of wilderness life and lacked his willingness to present human suffering and stoical endurance without qualification or didactic comment. Her sketch thus resolves into an encomium on the charity of supposedly enlightened men of modern civilization toward an unfortunate primitive race.

Annie's wilderness sketch may also have been inspired by another literary acquaintance, the young American realist Hamlin Garland, who arrived in Ottawa in December 1897 with a letter of introduction from his enthusiastic mentor, William Dean Howells. Garland had just returned from an arduous overland trek through British Columbia toward the Klondike, an expedition he was shortly to describe in a nostalgic prose narrative lament for the disappearing American frontier, *The Trail of the Gold Seekers* (1899), and he was full of stories about northern hardship and adventure. 'He is a lovely fellow,' Annie wrote Aurelia after meeting Garland, 'just as delightful as his stories.'[11]

Other notable literary figures found their way to the Fréchettes' New Edinburgh home with letters of introduction. In 1888, Achille's friend and former instructor at the Ottawa School of Art William Brymner presented a young 'Miss Duncan,' of Toronto, who was then writing for the Toronto *Star* under the name 'Garth Grafton.'[12] This was Sara Jeanette Duncan, one of the few Canadian disciples of Henry James and later author of the most important Canadian venture into the Jamesian realistic novel, *The Imperialist* (1904).

Pauline Johnson, the part-Mohawk princess and nature poet from Brantford, Ontario, was just beginning her career of lecture tours and recitals when she came to see the Fréchettes in Ottawa. Both she and Annie had probably known of each other for some years previous to their meeting: Pauline's mother, a sister-in-law of an Anglican missionary on the Brantford Six Nations reserve, was Emily Susanna Howells, a distant cousin of Annie's father. In the early stage of her career as lecturer and public reader, Pauline was reduced at one point to sending the Fréchettes an urgent request for financial assistance, upon which Achille commented, after sending the money: 'The poor thing has a hard time of it, I am afraid, and this life does her no good. She and a young Californian give a third-rate show in the small towns about the country, and don't do much for Art nor for themselves.'[13]

One of the most detailed records of the Fréchettes' literary friends and acquaintance concerns Achille's involvement with a group of French-Canadian poets who flourished in Ottawa in the 1890s. *Le Cercle des Dix*, of which Achille was one of the founders, was described by cultural historian James Le Moine:

I ... wrote [in 1893] to a literary friend, in Ottawa [i.e., Achille Fréchette], asking for particulars about the club, and in order to disclose its nature, shall now furnish an extract from his reply, 'We limit the club to ten members,' said he, 'though we have sometimes gone a little beyond – to keep it well in bounds. We invite to our meetings no outsiders, excepting an occasional distinguished stranger visiting Ottawa. We meet every Wednesday evening, at the house of one of the members ... At the close of each meeting the subject to be discussed at the next was chosen. No politics allowed; history, literature, archeology, fine arts, and sciences generally have their turn. A concise record of each sitting notes the proceedings.' Then follows a list of the Ottawa members for one meeting. 'Deville, A. Frechette, Hon. Telesphor Fournier, Alfred Garneau, A. Lusignan, Prevost, Sulte, Benoit.'[14]

Besides entertaining visitors and local literary figures in Ottawa, Annie and Achille were often able to provide Canadian literary figures with letters of introduction to take with them to the United States. The poet Wilfred Campbell, having joined the Ottawa literary circle by accepting a civil service sinecure in 1891, was entertained a few years later by William Dean Howells during a summer vacation in the States. 'The Campbells turned up at dinner-time,' Howells wrote Annie, 'and we fed them here. They are pleasant young people, and it was delightful to find a poet so full of poetry – *his* poetry. But he *is* a poet. *She* gave Elinor to know that you were valued in Ottawa for your own sake and not for your distinguished brother's!'[15]

Whether for their own sake or for the sake of their family connections, the Fréchettes definitely found themselves at the centre of a quite impressive local cultural circle. By 1890 their New Edinburgh home was a well established Ottawa salon, where distinguished individuals of both Canadian languages and from both Canada and the United States met for stimulating society. This social atmosphere must have served to compensate Annie for the rather frequent disappointments in her own literary career. If she was not quite the successful author she once dreamed of being, she was at least the friend and hostess of many famous writers who gladly accepted her congenial hospitality.

CHAPTER NINE

Later Years

As busy as she was with her various social and cultural activities, Annie managed to find time in the 1890s for another major literary project. After twenty years, she got out her copy of *Reuben Dale* and embarked on a thorough revision of the novel, with a view to trying again to have it published in book form. She improved the style throughout, and recalling William's complaints about the conclusion, she modified the insanity of her heroine to a temporary delirium, although she decided to retain the lightning-bolt death of Reuben Dale. After several months of tinkering with the novel, in the summer of 1894 she enlisted William's aid to find a publisher. Howells approached various companies, some of whom agreed to have a look at the manuscript, but one by one they all declined to bring it out as a book. Finally, after three years of submissions and rejections, William was forced to admit defeat. 'I am sending back poor Annie's manuscript,' he wrote Aurelia, '... it has been declined by Dodd & Mead, Appleton's, Harper's, Scribner's, and George Munro's Sons, and I can't now offer it anywhere else ... I know it is good, and if the times were good it could get a publisher.'[1]

The publishing business, like the North American economy as a whole, was in recession through much of the 1890s, but there were more than economic reasons for the failure of this refurbished version of *Reuben Dale*. Annie's stylistic revisions did not substantially alter the fact that the novel was, after all, twenty years old; in the interim, literary tastes and fashions had changed. In 1897 the kind of realism which William Dean Howells had pioneered was still widely practised, and Howells was still unquestionably one of the most successful and influential novelists in the United States. But there were many new writers on the scene, and although Howells tried his best to keep up with recent developments and was even noted for his public encouragement of young experimentalist talent, there was a constantly widening gap between his brand of realism and the work of such writers as Frank Norris, Stephen Crane, and Theodore Dreiser. The latter representatives of the new 'naturalist' movement were fundamentally disciples of Howells in their concern for social and psychological problems and their tendency to give dramatic priority to the observable surface of life. But Howells did not really sympathize with their interest in the scientific determinism of Darwin and Spencer, or with the explicitness in such matters as sex and violence which this determinism frequently entailed.

Howells' own steadily increasing concern for the problem of social justice had been climaxed by a powerful fictional study of class conflict, *A Hazard of New Fortunes* (1889); but his indomitable optimism had subsequently found expression in works which were to some extent literary curiosities, such as his mystical study of the unconscious, *The Shadow of a Dream* (1890), the Utopian fantasy *A Traveler from Altruria* (1894), or the nostalgic invocation of an earlier literary success, *Their Silver Wedding Journey* (1889). Until the end of his life, Howells would continue producing at least one novel a year, few of which show any substantial reduction in his immense creative energy. But as a new generation of writers emerged, it became increasingly clear that the Howells fictional idiom, to which *Reuben Dale* essentially belonged, was part of a vanishing era.

Paradoxically, however, the 1890s also saw the strenuous revival of an earlier literary fashion diametrically opposed to everything for which Howells' literary career stood. After years of vigorous attacks on the sentimental and melodramatic romance, Howells lived to watch in horror the resurgence of this genre in such best-selling swashbucklers as General Lew Wallace's *Ben Hur* (1880) and Charles Major's *When Knighthood Was in Flower* (1898). In English Canada as well as the United States the historical romance was popular. While Sara Jeanette Duncan's *The Imperialist* was largely ignored by the author's countrymen, Ontario-born Sir Gilbert Parker made a modest fortune with clumsily written Dumas imitations like *The Seats of the Mighty* (1896).

In the early twentieth century Howells was accused, somewhat unfairly, by young writers like Sinclair Lewis and Van Wyck Brooks of epitomizing an effete and decadent genteel tradition which stood for rather fastidious and aristocratic notions of art and society. Howells' art is too comprehensive to be assigned such reductive labels, but there can be no denying that in broad terms this genteel tradition existed, and if it was not consciously perpetuated by Howells himself it was preserved in the magazines he edited or wrote for, such as the *Atlantic* and *Harper's* and *Cosmopolitan*, and by lesser writers who considered themselves his associates or disciples. Editors like Henry Mills Alden of *Harper's* and Richard Watson Gilder of the *Century* belonged to a vanishing generation, and their literary periodical format was shortly to vanish with them, replaced especially after the First World War by the rotogravure and news magazine. Throughout her modest literary career, Annie Howells Fréchette had unquestionably belonged to this genteel school of writing, and she had neither the desire nor the ability to adapt to the new age. She would continue for several more years writing and publishing short stories in the 'genteel realist' vein, but the failure of the rewritten *Reuben Dale* clearly indicates not only her inherent limitations as a writer, but the obsolescence of the literary values to which she subscribed.

Much the same sort of commentary could be applied to the tradition of French-Canadian literature in which Louis and Achille Fréchette had been nurtured. In the 1890s, the nationalist-romantic school of Quebec writers was still comparatively popular, by virtue of the fact that patriotic sentiments in French-Canadian literature were never completely out of fashion. Louis Fréchette had, in fact, just recently achieved his most splendid popular and critical success with a sequence of patriotic poems, *La Légende d'un Peuple* (1887). But a generation of writers who still looked back to Hugo and Lamartine for inspiration inevitably began to sound antiquated, especially in contrast with the work of young members of the Ecole littéraire de Montréal such as the brilliant and unstable Emile Nelligan. Inspired by Baudelaire and the French symbolists, and indirectly by the dark and brooding imaginations of the American romantics Melville, Hawthorne, and Poe, Nelligan and his cohorts moved away from patriotism toward a more painful exploration of the individual psyche. Louis Fréchette's rather noisily dramatic exile thus was replaced by a plaintive and moody introvert meditating on his existence not merely as a *canadien errant*, but as a wanderer over the mystifying and frightening landscape of the whole universe. The older generation of French-Canadian romantics had, furthermore, over the years taken rather frequently to distasteful public squabbles scarcely designed to improve their reputations. Louis Fréchette had been involved in charges and counter-charges of plagiarism and, having satirically attacked some of his literary friends in *Originaux et Détraqués: Douze Types québécois* (1892), was excoriated in turn by an old friend, francophone poet William Chapman, in *Le Lauréat* (1894).

It is interesting to observe as indicative of this transitional literary era that in the 1890s both William Dean Howells and Louis Fréchette began to make nostalgic public reviews of their lives and careers. The first of several volumes of reminiscences, Howells' *A Boy's Town*, appeared in 1890, and Fréchette's *Mémoires intimes* was serialized in *Le Monde illustré* in 1900. Both writers, as they approached their sixtieth birthdays, were inevitably becoming more conscious of the passage of time, and their mood was frequently reflective, egocentric, nostalgic. Achille and Annie Fréchette were likewise conscious of the passing years. In 1899 Achille published a poem in *Le Passe-Temps* entitled 'J'ai Cinquante Ans!' and although the poem was intended as a public birthday gift for a friend, Achille had himself reached the half-century mark two years earlier, and must have inevitably been expressing his identification and sympathy with the recipient. Not that the occasion called for any admission of regret: 'J'ai Cinquante Ans!' is a gay, exuberant song, in which the speaker, like Achille himself with his persistent eye trouble, regrets nothing but his fading eyesight:

> Trinquons amis et le cœur en liesse
> De la gaîte rompons le 'pain bénit'!
> Nous enterrons cinquante ans de jeunesse
> Mais le bon temps n'est pas encor fini.
> Allez les voix rires et chanson nettes!
> Comme autrefois le bon vieux Béranger,
> 'J'ai cinquante ans et je porte lunettes,'
> Il faut au moins un peu se déranger.[2]

But in spite of the optimism and natural zest for life which enabled them to adapt to the passing years, Achille and Annie Fréchette could not help but be conscious of the rapid changes marking the virtual disappearance of the world of their youth. Annie was particularly conscious of how much history she had seen when she wrote Aurelia on 10 June 1891: 'We – the children and I – are at Achille's office, where we have been since eleven o'clock to see Sir John Macdonald's funeral ... We are waiting to see the procession come back from St. Alban's church – it is to pass along Wellington Street, to the CPR station, en route to Kingston.' And a few hours later, she resumed the letter: 'I was anxious to see how this funeral compared with that of Lincoln, which you know I saw at Columbus. While it was conducted officially, it had almost none of the characteristics of a public funeral. Of course the military and different societies were out; still there was all the quiet and decorum of a private burial – not a flag or a banner to be seen along the whole line.'[3]

The 1890s also brought personal bereavement, and a rupture of the most important link with Annie's Ohio girlhood, when William Cooper Howells died on 28 August 1894, at the age of eighty-seven. For the previous eight years, since William Cooper had given up the Virginia farm, Annie had spent part of almost every summer in Jefferson, sometimes accompanied by her two children, helping Aurelia to look after their ailing father and their mentally retarded brother Henry. Annie's two older brothers Joseph and Sam remained in Jefferson for the rest of their lives, and Annie continued to make her annual summer visits to Ohio until 1902, when Aurelia moved to Ottawa with Henry; but after the death of her father she must have felt that the Ohio portion of her life had drawn to an irrevocable close.

There was compensation, however, for these sad public and private events, in corresponding happy developments. In 1896, five years after the death of Macdonald, the Liberals finally came back into power under Wilfrid Laurier, thus promising a new era of prosperity for long-standing party supporters such as Achille Fréchette. And in their private lives, the Fréchettes were gratified by the achievements of their children, both of whom as they approached adulthood showed signs of exceptional promise. Their son Howells had early revealed an aptitude for scientific studies, in which he was enthusiastically encouraged by his parents. In 1901 he graduated from McGill University, taking a B SC with high honours in metallurgy, and went on to a long and distinguished career first in the mining industry and subsequently with the Department of Mines in Ottawa. Their daughter Marie-Marguérite followed a little more closely in her parents' professional footsteps. Eventually, after studying in New York and Paris, she was able to make a modest living as a portrait artist.

As far as public life was concerned, the cultural and social prestige enjoyed by Achille and Annie Fréchette in Canada continued to increase steadily throughout the 1890s. From 1892 to 1902, Achille served on the French editorial committee of the *Transactions of the Royal Society of Canada*; from 1893 to 1898, he was secretary of the Ottawa Art Association. Under Laurier's Liberals, he was made acting chief translator of the House of Commons in 1902, and the following year he was confirmed in the permanent appointment to the position. On her part,

Annie received comparable public distinction. After 1893, she found herself in the social circle of Lady Aberdeen, wife of the new governor-general. Unlike most of their predecessors, Lord and Lady Aberdeen were Liberals in politics and comparatively democratic in their social relationships. Lady Aberdeen especially, who by all accounts was the more socially aggressive of the two, admitted many Canadian Liberal supporters to her social circle; she was active in the establishment of various local and national causes, and in finding preferment for her friends. Shortly after her arrival in Canada, she established the National Council of Women, to which Annie Fréchette was named corresponding secretary of the Ottawa branch. In 1897, she helped found the Victorian Order of Nurses in Canada, of which Annie was also appointed to the local committee.

As the 1890s drew to a close, the Fréchettes could mark many changes not only in their personal and public lives, but in their environment as well. Ottawa, like Canada – like the western world as a whole – had altered remarkably in the last quarter of the nineteenth century. The city's population had more than doubled since the Fréchettes first arrived, from the twenty thousand of 1877 to about fifty thousand in 1900. The rough dirt-and-gravel streets which became bogs of mud during the spring and fall rains were partially macadamized, at least in the commercial districts of the city; and in the downtown and better residential districts the wooden sidewalks had been replaced by concrete. In 1877, the small business district was clustered near the unfinished Parliament Buildings, and comprised only a few low, narrow concrete and brick commercial blocks, along with many less solid looking structures often hastily constructed of the cheap and plentiful locally sawn lumber.

By the turn of the century, the downtown core extended in several directions from the riverfront, along Bank and Sparks and Elgin streets, and featured many multi-storeyed brick and stone buildings with the rows of closely set tall arched windows, pseudo-Gothic friezes, gables, and truncated towers which passed in the Victorian age for architectural elegance. By 1900, electric lights, telephones, and electric streetcars were common features of the capital. With the new century, the city's first horseless carriages made their appearance. Ottawa was not, in the 1890s or at any time in the nineteenth century, an attractive city: it was too subject to the evolutions and convolutions of progress, too incongruous in its violent yoking of disparate elements, to have much aesthetic appeal. But the noisy and swarming activity of the sawmills along the river below Parliament Hill, juxtaposed to the façade of British calmness and orderliness suggested by the Parliament Buildings, combined with the busy economic and social life of the burgeoning city, all proclaimed Ottawa's allegiance to the main articles of secular faith professed by the Victorian age.

The closing years of the century found the Fréchettes busy as usual, Achille with his duties as chief translator and with occasional journalism, and Annie with her writing, her club and committee work, and travelling. In 1897 another public debate broke out between the two political factions represented by *Le Temps* and *Le Canada*, this one a rather sordid and pathetic sequel to the death of Achille's old friend and former editor of *Le Temps*, Oscar McDonnell. McDonnell, in the suffering of his final illness, had apparently been persuaded by his 'spiritual advisor' to sign a statement admitting guilt for any sins he *might* have committed against the proper authority of the church. The ultramontane newspapers *Le Manitoba* and *Le Canada* gloatingly interpreted this statement as a confession of specific guilt for McDonnell's involvement in anti-clerical causes such as the attack on the separate schools. After condemning the ecclesiastics and their editorial supporters for their 'cruauté sans nom faite à un pauvre mourant,' Achille ridiculed them for their cowardice and hypocrisy. The ultramontanists were unable to argue effectively against McDonnell while he was alive, Achille charged, because he knew more true Catholic doctrine than they did; hence, they were reduced to attacking him when he was dying and dead: 'On a l'hypocrisie, la malhonnêteté de parler d'erreur doctrinale. ... Oscar McDonnell ... était trop prudent pour jamais s'aventurer, sans être dix fois sûr de lui, sur un terrain où un simple faux pas eût été la ruine de son journal et de sa cause. Parlez d'erreurs doctrinales à Ottawa, et vous ferez sourire bien du monde, qui savent dans quel pétrin certaines gens auraient fait engager les autorités diocésaines, si la sagesse de celles-ci ne les avait protégées contre les impatiences moins éclairées de leur entourage.'[4]

But these public quarrels were taking their toll on Achille's nerves and physical health, especially when they occurred during the Liberal administration, while the civil service was undergoing new reform and expansion and Achille's professional responsibilities were steadily increasing. The Oscar McDonnell affair, which was obviously a very painful business, was Achille's last foray into newspaper debating.

Annie, meanwhile, was equally busy. In 1899 Louis Fréchette enlisted her editorial assistance in the preparation of his one book written in English, a collection of local colour sketches and folk tales, *Christmas in French Canada*. Annie apparently read the preface and some of the stories, and offered suggestions for improving the phrasing and diction.[5] In February 1900 she scored another minor journalistic success with a brief article in the *Century*, 'A Banner Divorce County,' on the unusually high divorce rate in Ashtabula County, Ohio. And in January 1901, Annie spent a month in New York City, where Vevie was now studying at the same Art Students' League school which her father had attended some eighteen years earlier. William Dean Howells was now living in New York, where he had moved in 1891 to serve briefly as the editor of *Cosmopolitan* and subsequently to continue his career as a novelist.

The most exciting of the first years of the new century for Annie, however, was probably 1906. Vevie, having finished her studies in New York the previous summer, was working in her own portrait studio in Ottawa. William Dean Howells, after many years of unavoidable postponements and abortive intentions, finally visited his sister and her husband in the Canadian capital. And also in 1906 Annie unexpectedly received an opportunity to make an extensive journey across western Canada.

The trans-Canada trip came as the result of an invitation from the Canadian Women's Press Club, which was holding its annual meeting in Winnipeg. Annie had been recommended to the club's executive as a likely member, not only because of her reputation as a journalist and feature writer for magazines, but also because she seemed especially qualified to participate in a project which the club had recently undertaken. The Western Canadian Immigration Association had offered to underwrite the travel expenses of a selected group of presswomen for an extended trip through the prairie provinces; these individuals would in return write articles publicizing the attractions of the western provinces for prospective immigrants and developers. Annie understandably leaped at the chance of this free excursion, especially since it offered her the opportunity to visit her son Howells, who was working as a mining engineer at Fernie, in southern British Columbia near the Alberta border. So after making arrangements to submit her travel articles to several American newspapers, Annie set out for Winnipeg.

Such publicity schemes as this of the Western Canadian Immigration Association were fairly common in the early years of the twentieth century. The Dominion government as well as private land speculators were eagerly promoting the settlement and agricultural development of Manitoba, Saskatchewan, and Alberta, which had become, since the virtual disappearance of free or cheap land in the western United States, the 'last, best west' in the popular imagination as well as in the economic and demographic structures of North America. So the

Canadian Women's Press Club was only one of dozens of publicity outlets enlisted in the cause of promoting the Canadian West.

It is a subject of interesting speculation, however, whether the two parties involved in this particular promotional scheme were entirely aware of the affinities of each other. The Western Canadian Immigration Association, in spite of its official-sounding name, was actually a consortium of private American land speculators and developers with headquarters in Minneapolis, devoted to the encouragement of American immigration and investment in the Canadian prairies.[6] Most of the members of the Canadian Women's Press Club, in contrast, were passionate Canadian imperialists, devoted to the preservation of British traditions and loyalty to the Empire in Canada, and to the resistance of American cultural and economic influences.

The president of the club was the ardent imperialist Mrs Theodore Coleman of Toronto, who wrote under the pen-name 'Kit' for the equally ardent imperialist newspaper, the Toronto *Mail and Empire*. Mrs Coleman was largely responsible for a series of nine letters published in that paper during July and August 1906, entitled 'What a Woman Saw in the West,' chronicling the travels of the delegates from Winnipeg to Edmonton and back. Most of the letters are strenuously opposed to the importation of American customs and institutions to the Canadian West. Observing to her horror an American flag erected on the Edmonton city hall by some overenthusiastic American immigrants on the fourth of July, the series writer indignantly wrote: 'The flag of Empire should be the only flag to fly from a Canadian city's hall. If we do not honour our own country, who will? Of what use our St. George's societies, our Daughters of the Empire chapters, if not to nurture and cherish those things that old Britain gave us?'[7]

Significantly, however, the first letter of the series, immediately preceding the one just quoted, takes an entirely different tone from all the others. In a passage obviously designed to please the sponsors of the excursion, the author refers to 'the Western Canadian Immigration Association, a company which is doing broad and fine work for western Canada.' And after describing the endless construction and the thriving wheat farms along the railway route to Edmonton, the writer concludes: 'The whole west is booming like a great hive ... Edmonton strikes you at once as a very substantial reality. The long irregular main street fairly hums with business. American enterprise is keen in the place, and Americans are well liked for their sharp business methods, their friendliness and the good citizens and settlers they make.'[8] The author of this first, unsigned letter in the *Mail and Empire* was probably Annie Howells Fréchette. This probability is supported by the author's

passing comment that 'to me, alien-born, the thought that she, this big
Canada, was my more than foster land; that one had taken root in her,
and was the mother of children born on her soil, was in such a moment
a deep and touching thought.' If this author was Annie, her American
boosterism obviously did not appeal to her imperialistic colleagues like
Mrs Coleman, who promptly took over the *Mail and Empire* series,
leaving Annie to reserve her correspondence – no doubt to the greater
satisfaction of the Western Canadian Immigration Association – for
the American newspapers.

But Annie apparently did not allow any differences of political
opinion to detract from the pleasure of this western Canadian tour. 'We
have been following your flight with dazzled eyes across the continent,'
William wrote from New York, 'and I am glad to get a warbled note
from [you] in your perch at Fernie.'[9] In the British Columbia mining
town, Annie had a pleasant visit with her son, and out of curiosity and
nostalgia wrote to her employer of 1872, the Chicago *Inter-Ocean*, to ask
if they might be interested in a regular correspondence from Canada.
The editor of the *Inter-Ocean* replied that 'our publisher ... was much
interested in what I had to tell him of your early work in Chicago,' but
declined the proposed contribution on the grounds that a series from
British North America might prove offensive to their large contingent
of Irish-American readers.[10] Annie also began research for articles on
the Doukhobor settlements in Saskatchewan, and on American immigration to Canada. The western trip, like her first encounters with New
England and eastern Canada many years before, was opening up a
great variety of new experience and literary opportunity. But Annie
was thirty years older: in the 1870s, her enthusiasm could be readily
turned into literary productivity; in 1906, it was all she could do to keep
up the newspaper articles she had contracted to write on her western
tour. Most of her projects to develop western topics into feature articles
remained unfinished; and at the end of August she returned home to
Ottawa, exhilarated but exhausted.

There was not much time to rest, however, because William Dean
Howells had finally declared his intention to visit Ottawa, and was
expected to arrive in mid-September. Howells could only spend a few
days in Canada, but Annie wanted to make sure that he would leave
with a completely favourable impression of the capital city and its
society. It appears that the novelist had no clear idea of the Fréchettes'
rank in Canadian social and official circles, so the visit came as an
extremely pleasant surprise for him. At his sister's table, he found
himself rubbing elbows with Prime Minister Laurier and the Anglican

Bishop of Ottawa. 'I have begun to tell Elinor about the reception and the dinner,' he wrote Annie after his return to New York, 'and her excitement has been all that I prophesied. She is fully as much impressed with my meeting Laurier as I could wish, and she has again pronounced him the greatest of possible statesmen.'[11]

Howells also set to work on a brief article on Ottawa for the 'Editor's Easy Chair' department of *Harper's*, which he had been writing regularly since 1899. The article begins with a general complaint about the widespread indifference to Canada in the United States – 'the cultivated American who is keenly alive to the existence of a dominion bordering us beyond the seas, is comparatively dead to the presence of a Dominion bordering us beyond the lakes and rivers' – and goes on to describe the social and cultural potential of the 'Washington of the north.' This label, which was coined by Sir Wilfrid Laurier, conveys an implicit image of Canada as a rival or imitation of the United States, an impression to which Howells contributes by contending that 'we made [Canada's] opportunity possible through our suffering and revolt.' But his Ottawa article is actually concerned with Canada's potential as an alternative to American republicanism:

Is it a fancy that the air, yonder, the pure air of a climate when it is as cold half the year as if liquefied, is less haunted than ours with the giant forms of the Trusts and Distrusts which threaten our peace? ... No doubt, if we could look into the heart of the neighboring power, we should see the like of the bitterness which stirs in our own, the commercial lust, the industrial unrest ... This is something which teases the thought of the witness from time to time, and which he can only put aside by answering his own question with the fact that it [the Canadian social system] works. How long it will work no one can say, for no one can calculate the lifetime of an anomaly.[12]

Significantly, this essay on Ottawa echoes at various points one of Howells' earliest pieces of writing on Canada, the travelogue novel *Their Wedding Journey* (1872), a fact which suggests that after the northern trip of 1906 he spent some time rereading his early work and rethinking his attitudes to Canada of thirty years earlier, possibly under the influence of table-talk with his brother-in-law and Sir Wilfrid Laurier. In *Their Wedding Journey*, he had condemned the neither fish nor fowl atmosphere of Canada resulting from its persistent loyalty to England: 'The American traveller,' he said in that novel, '[feels] like saying to the hulking giant beyond St. Lawrence and the Lakes, "sever the apron strings of allegiance, and try to be yourself, whatever you are."' In the prose sketch of 1906, however, he acknowledges that Canada, as 'an independent dominion in dependence on an inclusive empire,' has successfully managed 'to throw off the guidance of the Mother Country, without apparently severing the political ties which one need not be so offensive as to call apron strings.'[13]

Besides leading to a reconsideration of his ideas on the political institutions of Canada, Howells' visit inspired a more extensive and more personal literary project. In April 1907, he wrote his friend Charles Eliot Norton that he had been working 'at odd times during the winter on a longish, slowish sort of New England idyl which I call *The Children of the Summer.*'[14] According to a comment of Howells' daughter Mildred, who edited his *Life in Letters*, this title refers to the novel which was eventually published after Howells' death as *The Vacation of the Kelwyns*. This novel, concerning the visit of a young girl to the summer home of her relatives the Kelwyns in the Centennial summer of 1876, is of course based on Annie's visit with her brother and sister-in-law thirty years earlier, just before she agreed to marry Achille Fréchette. Confronted by the spectacle of his sister's brilliant social position in Ottawa, Howells turned imaginatively to the past, as he was more and more inclined to do in old age, to that summer when the future for his sister, for himself, for all North America in the depths of an economic depression seemed so uncertain.

The Vacation of the Kelwyns, like Shakespeare's *Tempest*, is an expression of reconciliation and contentment, ending with marriage for the young heroine and a benign acceptance of the uncertain conditions of life for her older cousin Kelwyn, who obviously reflects aspects of the character of Howells himself. But this novel deals primarily with the positive and idealistic side of Howells' attitudes late in life; it does not indicate the negative experiences of disappointment, bereavement, sense of unachieved possibilities, and especially of declining physical capacities which are inevitable features of old age. Howells himself at sixty-nine in 1906 was in reasonably good health, and was to live fourteen more years, although many of his closest literary friends and acquaintances were gone. Most distressing for him was the illness of his wife Elinor, who had been too weak to make the trip to Ottawa, and who was to live, a semi-invalid, for only four more years.

In Canada, the Fréchettes were equally made aware of the inexorable passage of time. Louis Fréchette, aged sixty-seven in 1906, was in poor health; the following year, he and his wife retired to an apartment in the Institut des Sourdes-Muettes in Montreal, where Louis as a semi-invalid could have virtually constant medical supervision. In

April 1908, he suffered a stroke. Achille, hurrying to Montreal upon receiving the news, wrote to Annie: 'My poor brother passed away an hour after I arrived – he had not recovered consciousness and died in that condition. He had been struck by an apoplexy at about a quarter past ten Saturday night (exactly 24 hours before his death), at the foot of the steps of the Hospice where he lived, and remained under a beating rain until he was found lying there two hours afterward. But the poor fellow of course did not suffer.'[15] Achille and Louis Fréchette had had their differences over the years, but in spite of their occasional alienation, Achille could not help but recall their childhood and youth together, their sojourn as semi-bohemian literary exiles in Chicago during the 1870s, and Louis' indisputable leadership of the nationalistic French-Canadian literary movement in which Achille played a minor part.

Achille himself was not in good health by 1908. He was showing definite symptoms of heart trouble, and every year the severe Ottawa winters took their toll on his weakening constitution. On several occasions he considered the possibility of an early retirement, but there were many factors to take into account, including the economic problems involved in living on a severely limited income. But in 1909 an opportunity came his way to make a tentative experiment with semi-retirement and to travel to a more moderate climate. The House of Commons, through the Board of Internal Economy, was interested in making a comparative investigation of translation methods, with a view to improving its own translation office. Achille was the logical person to undertake this investigation, which would involve the study of translation services in the two most prominent European countries with bilingual and multilingual parliaments, Belgium and Switzerland. This part-time research project could be combined with an extended leave of absence, during which Achille could decide whether he was willing or able to continue his professional duties. Annie would stay in Ottawa while Achille completed the official part of his European trip; then if he decided to take his retirement she could join him. Vevie was already in Europe: early in 1909 she had set out to tour England and France, and to study art in Paris, so Achille would have company for some of his travels and residence abroad. Leaving his office in the hands of his assistant translator and long-time friend Emery Perrin, in January 1910 Achille set sail for France.

CHAPTER TEN

Final Years:
Europe and America

In October 1910 the King's Printer in Ottawa published a *Report on the Enquiry Requested by the Board of Internal Economy of the House of Commons of Canada to be Made in Belgium and Switzerland*, dealing with 'the organization and working of the systems of translation obtaining in those [countries].' This report, published simultaneously in English and French versions, both written by Achille Fréchette, is not a landmark work in the long and troubled history of bilingualism and biculturalism in Canada, but as a minor contribution to this perennial Canadian controversy, it deserves brief comment.

The author's main concern is with the modernization of a system which has failed to keep pace with the proliferation and diversification of government services. The report has three sections, and three sets of recommendations, dealing with the translation of parliamentary debates, sessional papers (proceedings of the various government departments), and legislation. In the translation of parliamentary debates, Fréchette suggests that Canada should follow the example of Belgium, where speeches are published in full in their original language of delivery and in résumé in the other language. For the sessional papers, each government department in Belgium and Switzerland has its own translation staff, in contrast to the system in Canada, where the House of Commons office has to handle all public reports from all departments:

The present system, established some fifty years ago, may have answered the needs of the time, when the public documents were very far from being as voluminous, as numerous and as specialized as they are today, and when the greater part of them, being already in French, had not to go through the

French Office. But now that the publications of the public service deal with so many activities unknown to the primitive country that we were then; now that all the human interests, more and more specialized, find their expression in the papers presented to the Canadian parliament, a centralized translation office can no longer do justice to so much work that calls for specialists. The experience I have acquired during thirty-six years of service in the Commons has convinced me that in centralization rests the vice of our system.[1]

Finally, the translation of laws, currently handled by the House of Commons office regardless of which house originated the legislation, should be undertaken by a joint office for Commons and Senate, as in Belgium and Switzerland.

The first recommendation, to publish résumés of Commons speeches in the language other than that of delivery, was by far the most controversial. The great majority of speeches in the Commons were delivered in English, so most of the résumés obviously would be French summaries of English speeches. In effect, such a system would have been an indirect but distinct step towards giving the French language a subordinate place in the Canadian parliamentary system. Achille Fréchette must surely have recognized the implications of this recommendation, but apparently his attitude to the official use of the two Canadian languages still reflected those assumptions about utilitarian education instilled in him by his early teachers.

This recommendation, which probably would have proved offensive to most francophone members of Parliament, was never adopted. Indeed, like many similar parliamentary documents, Achille Fréchette's report on translation services, after one reprinting (in 1920), virtually disappeared in the morass of bureaucratic publications, and none of his recommendations was ever put into effect. Instead of following the pattern of decentralization presented by Belgium and Switzerland, the Canadian Parliament preferred to rely on expansion of the central translation office to deal with the continual proliferation of government services.

After completing the report, Achille made a definite decision to take his retirement, so the study of translation systems in Belgium and Switzerland was the last official act of a long and distinguished civil service career. Shortly after his arrival in Europe, the process of official recognition of this career had been set in motion when a group of friends recommended Achille to Sir Wilfrid Laurier as a potential recipient of the Imperial Service Order, a medal for distinguished service awarded to civil servants in the British Empire. His career, in effect, had thus come full circle: like his hero of many years before, Louis-Joseph Papineau, Achille found himself being honoured late in life by those very institutions and traditions against which his youthful self had rebelled. In 1874 he had renounced his allegiance to the British queen and had almost become an American citizen; in 1910 his name was on the honours list of His Majesty King George the Fifth.

While Achille was completing his report, Annie was busy back in Ottawa preparing to join her husband in Switzerland, where they had decided to begin their retirement. Her sister Aurelia was now living with her, and since their mentally retarded brother Henry had died in 1908, Aurelia's long domestic responsibility had ended and she was planning to join the Fréchettes in Switzerland. Before they could embark for Europe, however, word came from the United States of new family sorrow: in May 1910, Elinor Mead Howells died. Annie and Aurelia at once left for New York City, and after the funeral they spent part of the summer with William Dean Howells in his Maine summer home. Finally, in the autumn of 1910, Annie and Aurelia sailed for Europe.

The Fréchettes and Aurelia settled in Lausanne, Switzerland, where they were joined by Marie-Marguérite after she had finished her art studies in Paris. While Achille devoted himself to sketching, painting, and scholarly study, Annie wrote occasional short stories, although her success with publication continued to be mixed. She tried her hand at two stories set in Switzerland, one a sentimental tale of love, 'Sweet Sings the Nightingale,' and the other an attempt at realism, 'On the Mountain Side,' which juxtaposes alpine scenery with a sordid tale of drunkenness and violence among Swiss cottagers. Both tales, however, were declined by her old friend, H.M. Alden of *Harper's*. 'The pictures of alpine life and scenery in your story "On the Mountain Side" are admirable,' he wrote, 'but the story is too unrelievedly gloomy in its conclusion.' Concerning the love story, Alden confessed himself 'old-fashioned enough to like [it], though the new generation discourages this older vein. I should like some fiction from you meeting our more modern need and mood.'[2]

A third story, however, had better luck. 'His First-Born' (*McClure's*, September 1912), about a repentant young father who goes in search of his half-Indian illegitimate child, attempts to deal with a modern, or at least a controversial, theme and no doubt the references to illegitimacy and miscegenation are what caught the *McClure's* editors' attention. But like the treatment of adultery in *Reuben Dale*, these subjects are dealt with very circumspectly, and resolved with a similar insistence on stereotyped moral judgments. One character in the story is described as 'the worst type of that half-breed which comes from a worthless white man who is too lazy or too dishonest to live among his own people, and who sinks below the people of his wife.'[3] But the half-breed child in the story is saved precisely because his father is not this kind of white man, but is rather the decent, conventional romantic hero of popular fiction.

Although this was by no means Annie's last written work, it was to be her last published work of fiction. The changes in taste and in artistic attitudes which were clearly discernible by the turn of the century were proceeding at an accelerated rate, and shortly there would be the great aesthetic revolution following in the wake of the social and political upheaval of the First World War. Annie's antiquated brand of genteel realism, which depended too heavily on stereotypes and supposedly self-evident moral and psychological assumptions, was no longer a viable fictional medium. The *McClure's* editors asked for a sequel to 'His First-Born,' but when Annie submitted 'His Mother and His Wife,' it was declined. 'It was shabby of McClures to get you to do that sequel and then refuse it,' William wrote sympathetically.[4] But this editorial indecision was symptomatic of the changes taking place in literature which were only dimly understood even by those who were in presumed control of the literary media.

Annie's last ambitious – and uncompleted – literary project was undertaken in 1913, while she was on a visit home to North America. Achille's indifferent health prevented him from accompanying her, but Annie spent several weeks with her son Howells, now an official in the Department of Mines at Ottawa, and with her brother William, down in New York. While in Ottawa, she collected fifteen of her stories, including some unpublished as well as previously published pieces, and began revising and arranging them for a proposed volume. The manuscript, however, was never finally prepared for the press. That the project was left incomplete was probably just as well, because it would surely have led to disappointment, if not from the inherent weakness or obsolescence of her fictional idiom, then certainly from the intervention of world affairs, which were shortly to disrupt the cultural and social life of virtually the whole of western civilization.

The war broke out while the Fréchettes and Aurelia were living at Lausanne, and since they could have no idea of the duration of the conflict, they decided to await further developments before making a decision about returning to America. Eventually, they waited too long, until the submarine warfare made the Atlantic crossing too great a risk to be undertaken by three elderly people, and they were compelled to wait out the war in Switzerland. Achille's declining health, combined with the official restrictions on travel, drastically limited the Fréchettes' activities, but they managed to endure the war with their usual patience and cheerfulness. A summary of their wartime life is contained in a letter from Annie to a distant cousin, the minor American playwright Paul Kester:

Once in a long time we get hold of an American book, but our reading is chiefly of this tedious war, the end of which is not yet in sight. We feel sadly cut off from home here, on this little inland island of peace, for it is next to impossible to get off it. But we are thinking seriously of trying a flight to Italy as the prospect of a coal-less winter in Switzerland is not an alluring one for a rheumatic and not over-strong family. Still we are uncertain about that – just as we are about everything else these days. We are here [at Zurich] for a few weeks on our way back from a series of baths at Ragaz – near the Austrian frontier. That is, my husband and my sister and I are here. Vevie stayed behind in Lausanne as she dislikes German-Switzerland and also because she is a very busy girl these days, painting, going more deeply into French, learning Italian, and filling in such chinks in time left in doing what she can for interned, invalid, and crippled soldiers in the way of writing them letters or reading to those whose sight is impaired ...

Although we see no present prospect of getting back to America, that does not deter us from making plans or dreaming dreams ... We came to Europe thinking to spend only months here, but each month has been turned into a year. My husband was sent over by the Canadian government to study and report upon the system of translation in use in Belgium and Switzerland where they have the same problem of several languages to deal with that we have in Canada, and after making the report he asked for his retirement, as after nearly forty years of service in the Translation Branch, of which he had become the head, had quite worn him out [sic]. And so we stayed on until caught here by the war, after which we had not the courage to face the new perils of the sea.

We long to get back to America as soon as it is safe to go, but the question always asks itself, 'where shall we settle?' My husband was very ill two years ago, with heart weakness, and at that time the Swiss doctor who brought him safely through, said he would not again be able to endure the severe cold of Canadian winters. So, though we would naturally return to Ottawa, because our son Howells is in the government there, we dare not take the risk. We have thought seriously of Washington, or rather its vicinity. In Lausanne we have several friends from Maryland who have held out tempting prospects there. But they have been long away and conditions have doubtless changed.[5]

Achille's health continued poor, curtailing his artistic activities, but he found time and energy for some writing of poetry, including two sonnets which he had printed and sent as New Year's greetings to various Canadian friends in 1917. The two poems are rather old-fashioned lyric evocations of setting and mood, reflecting nothing of the contemporary world crisis, but recalling the nature descriptions of his early success, 'Les Martyrs de la Foi au Canada.' As specimens of this nineteenth-century French lyrical tradition, they are among the best of Achille's writings, and deserve to be quoted:

Au Pied des Alpes

Flots frappés qui alliez faire l'assaut des cieux!
Témoins restés debout des temps géologiques!
Drapés dans votre orgueil comme des dieux antiques
Portant jusqu'à l'éther leurs fronts impérieux.

Combien à votre tour, combien d'audacieux
Rêves d'escalader vos masses titaniques
N'avez-vous pas punis en vos gestes tragiques
   Ô monts prodigieux!

Mais si les aigles seuls là-haut trouvent des aires,
Plus près de nous, pourtant, vous êtes tutélaires:
Vos bois ont le gibier, vos vallons ont le miel,
Vos coteaux le vin d'or, et vos grasses prairies,
D'un peuple sage et bon, libre, béni du ciel,
Nourrissent les troupeaux dans des herbes fleuries.

La Sirène de l'Alpe

Sac au dos, pieds ferrés, alpenstock à la main,
Le touriste a marché depuis avant l'aurore.
Vers le sommet lointain qu'un soudain soleil dore,
Lentement il se fraye un pénible chemin
Par la falaise à pic, l'arête, le ravin,
Escaladant, rampant, glissant, montant encore,
Vaincant mille dangers que son audace ignore;
Dans une heure il vivra son rêve souverain!

Mais voici qu'il a vu, dans une touffe verte, –
Ô tragique attirance! – une édelweiss ouverte.
Il la veut; et l'abîme est là béant sans lui ...

Fatalité? – Non pas! Sur la sinistre roche,
Cette étoile-fleur dont l'étrange rayon luit,
C'est un phare qui du péril défend l'approche.[6]

After the armistice the Fréchettes went back to France to allow
Achille further rest in his recurring heart trouble, and to avoid the first
post-war rush of trans-Atlantic tourism; finally, in the summer of 1919
they sailed for Canada. Most of the next two years were spent in
Ottawa, renewing old acquaintances and enjoying the company of
their son Howells, his wife, and their two grandsons, born during the
war. In November 1919, Annie read a descriptive paper on Switzerland to a public gathering in Ottawa, and Achille published one of his
last poems, a descriptive lyric 'Chanson d'Automne,' which was set to
music and translated into English verse by Annie's old friend from the
Youth's Companion, now a journalist in Ottawa, Edward William Thomson.[7]

Post-war North America had changed almost beyond recognition,
and nowhere were the changes more evident than in Ottawa. The most
dramatic change involved the Parliament Buildings, which had been
almost completely destroyed by fire in 1916, and although they were
being rebuilt in almost the same Gothic design, the massive activity of
construction on Parliament Hill was symptomatic of the virtual renova-
tion of the city. The population was now over one hundred thousand,
and automobiles had almost completely replaced the horse and car-
riage on the streets. The first inter-city radio broadcast in Canada was
demonstrated in Ottawa in 1920; the city's first airport was opened in
the same year. All these signs of the new age of technology were for
people of the Fréchettes' generation inevitable indications of the passing of their own era. But the definitive mark of the end of an era, for
Annie and Achille, came in May 1920, with the news of the death of
William Dean Howells in New York, at the age of eighty-three. After
the funeral Annie set to work on what was to be her last publication, a
tribute to her brother's literary career, which appeared in the *Canadian
Bookman* in July 1920, consisting of reminiscences of their childhood
and youth and of Howells' interest in and writings on Canada.

As his Swiss doctor had warned, Achille could no longer endure the
severe Ottawa winters, and in the fall of 1921 the Fréchettes departed
for Victoria, British Columbia, in search of a milder climate. The
Vancouver Island air proved too damp, and early in 1922 they moved
south, settling finally in San Diego, California. In spite of the warmth
and sun and plentiful opportunities for rest, however, Achille's health

continued to fail. Finally, on 15 November 1927, one month and two days after his eightieth birthday, he died.

Annie, eighty-three years old at the time of her husband's death, and obviously possessed of the strong constitution of the generally long-lived Howells family, lived on for eleven more years. Although naturally stricken by the loss of her much-loved companion of more than half a century, she remained cheerful and active. She stayed on in San Diego with Aurelia and Marie-Marguérite, devoting her time to gardening, socializing, occasional rides in Vevie's new automobile, and reading. Still possessed of full mental and visual faculties, she tried to keep up with current literature, but the attempt was not wholly successful. Even Booth Tarkington's *Seventeen* (1916), surely a mild example of the work of the new literary generation in America, and written by a novelist whose technique and themes were similar to William Dean Howells' brand of realism, proved too psychologically explicit for her. 'No man,' her grandson recalls her saying of Tarkington's novel, 'should know that much about a woman's mind.'[8]

Much of her time was taken up with the continuation of her lifetime practice of writing long conversational letters to her many friends and relatives in the United States and Canada. Appropriately, considering her devotion to letter-writing, what might be considered her last public literary project involved serving as consultant on matters pertaining to the early years of the Howells family for her niece Mildred Howells' two-volume edition of the *Life in Letters of William Dean Howells* (1928). 'What a letter-writing family we have been,' Annie observed to her son Howells, as in 1936 she described her current attempts to sort through several bundles of family correspondence covering almost eighty years. 'In one pile there is considerably over a square foot – of open and flattened out letters from one alone, that have accumulated.'[9] The collection of letters continued to increase steadily, the outgoing correspondence decreasing as the immense burden of almost a century weighed upon the writer. Then at last, on 17 June 1938, the life of this cheerful, indefatigable, remarkable woman was at an end.

Notes

NOTES TO CHAPTER 1

1 Francis P. Weisenburger *The Passing of the Frontier* p. 81
2 Some of the details in the following summary of the Howells family background have been drawn from Edwin H. Cady *The Road to Realism*
3 'Incidents and Scenes for a Child's Story, Founded on Life at Eureka Mills,' ms draft (in possession of VDF). The idea for the story is also discussed in an unpublished letter, WDH to ATH, 26 Sept. 1867 (Houghton)
4 See WDH *Years of My Youth* p. 88, and compare Weisenburger *The Passing of the Frontier* p. 144
5 *Years of My Youth* p. 88
6 *Years of My Youth* p. 99
7 WDH *A Boy's Town* p. 21

8 WDH *My Literary Passions* pp. 38–9
9 Ms Diary of ATH (VDF)
10 See LF *Mémoires intimes* ed George A. Klinck chapter 10
11 Details of the elder Fréchettes and their natural and adopted children are in Lucien Serre *Louis Fréchette* pp. 164–91
12 Personal communication apparently dating from about 1922, from AF to Lucien Serre, quoted in Serre *Louis Fréchette* pp. 167–8
13 Serre pp. 184–5
14 AF to ATH, 6 Aug. 1876 (VDF)
15 Ibid.
16 Clipping from *Le Souvenir*, 1921 (VDF)
17 Certificate in possession of VDF
18 Mason Wade *The French-Canadian Outlook* p. 37
19 The curriculum of the Collège de Pointe-Lévy is described in Serre *Louis Fréchette* pp. 215–16

NOTES TO CHAPTER 2

1 See Cady *The Road to Realism* pp. 90–1
2 ATH to WDH, 16 March 1862 (VDF)
3 Lists of titles and rough draft of story in possession of VDF
4 WDH to ATH, 31 March 1861 (Houghton)
5 WDH to Aurelia Howells, 14 Jan. 1861 (VDF)
6 Ms Journal of ATH 1863–7 (VDF)
7 A collection of letters to ATH from various Union soldiers is in the Rutherford B. Hayes Library, Fremont, Ohio
8 Ms Journal of ATH 1863–7 (VDF)
9 WDH to ATH, 28 Jan. 1865 (Houghton)
10 EMH to ATH, 2 June 1867 (Houghton) mentions Longfellow's admiration for Annie, the inscribed copy of the poems is in the possession of VDF. Reference to the acquaintance with James, Dana, et al., is in ms journal of ATH 1863–7 (VDF); undated note, concerning attendance at concert, from Francis J. Child to ATH (Huntington); letters from H.H. Boyesen to ATH in possession of VDF
11 Ms Journal of ATH 1863–7 (VDF)
12 WDH to ATH, 26 Sept. 1867 (Houghton)
13 ATH to Mrs W.H. Smith, 19 Sept. 1867 (Ohio Historical Society)
14 William H. Smith to ATH, 3 April 1868 (VDF)
15 Details of the 1870 excursion to Niagara Falls and Canada are in a ms journal of the trip kept by ATH (VDF); correspondence about the respective plans of William and Annie to use the trip in fiction include WDH to ATH, 16 July 1871 and 6 March 1873 (Houghton)

16 WDH to ATH, 6 March 1873 (Houghton)
17 WDH to ATH, 27 May 1872 (Houghton)
18 ATH 'Fireworks' *The Galaxy* XIV (Sept. 1872) 398
19 EMH to ATH, 9 July [1872] (Houghton)
20 ATH to WDH, 17 Oct. 1877 (VDF)

NOTES TO CHAPTER 3

1 Quoted in Serre *Louis Fréchette* p. 174
2 'Les Martyrs de la Foi au Canada' *La Revue canadienne* (sept. 1868) 678–85
3 This poem, not published in the *Revue* until March 1871, is datelined by the author 'Québec, septembre, 1868'
4 The preceding outline of LF's early character and career is based on Serre *Louis Fréchette* and George A. Klinck *Louis Fréchette, prosateur*
5 Ms of poem in possession of VDF
6 LF 'A mon Frère Achille' *Poésies choisies* deuxième série p. 341
7 This portrait of Chicago in 1869 is based on Harold M. Mayer and Richard C. Wade *Chicago* pp. 35–73
8 See Klinck *Louis Fréchette* p. 28 for an account of the decline of *L'Amérique*
9 Achille's connection with 'la commerce des immeubles' is mentioned briefly in a page of autobiographical notes (VDF). His purchase of the Nebraska land is recorded in a ms notebook kept by him in 1873 (VDF)
10 AF to ATH, 25 June 1876 (VDF)
11 AF 'L'Irlande: Romance' *L'Opinion publique* II (19 oct. 1871) 504
12 Achille's Nebraska employment is mentioned briefly in the page of autobiographical notes (VDF)
13 The chronology of this early stage of Achille's Ottawa career is based on his autobiographical notes (VDF) and the back files of the *Courrier d'Outaouais* in the National Library, Ottawa. Details of the Canadian political scene in 1873–5 are based largely on Peter B. Waite *Canada 1874–1896* chapters 2 and 3

NOTES TO CHAPTER 4

1 WDH to ATH, n.d. [c. Aug. 1872] and 16 Nov. 1872 (Houghton)
2 She is thus described in an interview published in a San Diego, Calif., newspaper c. 1936 (undated clipping, VDF)
3 William's complaint and Annie's reply are referred to in letters from ATH to Aurelia Howells, n.d. [Feb. 1873?] (VDF), and WDH to ATH, 28 Feb. 1873 (Houghton)
4 William H. Smith to WDH, 31 Jan. 1873 (VDF)

5 Annie's intention to return to Jefferson and her father's response are indicated in WCH to ATH, 2 March 1873 (VDF)

6 WDH to ATH, 8 June 1873 (Houghton) and 27 July [1873] (VDF)

7 There is an extensive correspondence concerning Annie's attempts, and William's efforts on her behalf, to secure arrangements with various newspapers in 1873: George Cary Eggleston (editor of *Hearth and Home*) to WDH, 9 May 1873 (Huntington); WDH to ATH, 8 June 1873 (Houghton), 27 July [1873] (VDF), and 21 Oct. 1873 (Houghton); Eggleston to ATH, 26 Nov. 1873 (Houghton)

8 WDH to ATH, n.d. [c. March 1874?] (VDF)

9 Henry D. Thoreau *A Yankee in Canada* p. 13

10 Henry James 'Quebec' *Portraits of Places* p. 351

11 See especially Howells' travelogue novel *Their Wedding Journey* chapter 8

12 James 'Quebec' p. 355

13 James Le Moine *Maple Leaves, 7th Series* p. 365

14 Clipping from *Springfield Daily Union* 25 Aug. 1875 (Huntington). Gilman's identity as author of the article is confirmed by a letter from him to WCH, 27 Aug. 1875 (Huntington)

15 ATH 'Reuben Dale' *The Galaxy* xxi (April 1876) 511

16 'Reuben Dale' *The Galaxy* xx (Dec. 1875) 733

17 Nathaniel Hawthorne 'The Custom-House': Introductory to *The Scarlet Letter* Norton Critical Edition, ed Scully Bradley, Richard Croom Beatty, E. Hudson Long p. 31

18 WDH to Thomas S. Perry, 30 Oct. 1885 *Life in Letters of William Dean Howells* ed Mildred Howells I pp. 372–3

19 WDH to ATH, 24 Oct. 1874 (Houghton)

20 WDH 'The Smiling Aspects of American Life,' *William Dean Howells: Representative Selections* ed Clara M. Kirk and Rudolf Kirk p. 356

21 WDH to ATH, 24 Oct. 1874 (Houghton)

22 ATH 'Le Coureur des Bois' *Scribner's Monthly* xii (May 1876) 108–17. WDH's differences with Josiah Holland are outlined in Cady *The Road to Realism* pp. 122–5

NOTES TO CHAPTER 5

1 ATH to AF, 3 June 1876; AF to ATH, 11 June 1876 (VDF)

2 The documents relating to the courtship are all in the possession of VDF. They include a bundle of letters from AF to ATH, Feb.–Dec. 1876; a ms diary of ATH, Jan. 1876; LF to ATH, 18 Feb. 1876; ATH to LF, rough draft, n.d.; and ATH to EMH, 21 July 1876

3 ATH to EMH, 21 July 1876 (VDF)
4 WDH *The Vacation of the Kelwyns* p. 53
5 Ibid. pp. 55–6
6 AF to ATH, 11 March 1877 (VDF)
7 ATH to AF, 14 Oct. 1876 (VDF)
8 'Bibliographie' *Revue de Montréal* I (avril 1877) 187; 'Recent Literature' *Atlantic Monthly* XL (Sept. 1877) 377–8
9 H.M. Alden to ATH, 24 Jan. 1877 (Huntington). First draft of 'A Visit to a Country House' in possession of VDF
10 WDH to AHF, 20 July 1877 (Houghton)
11 Edmond's life and career are summarized in Serre *Louis Fréchette* pp. 169–73

NOTES TO CHAPTER 6

1 The historical facts, statistics, and some descriptive details about nineteenth-century Ottawa are based on Wilfrid Eggleston *The Queen's Choice* chapters 3–8, and Robert Haig *Ottawa* passim. The description of the Parliament Buildings skyline in the nineteenth century is in the words of a contemporary engineer with the Department of Public Works, quoted in Eggleston p. 128
2 AF to ATH, 6 Aug. 1876 (VDF)
3 See Alphonse Lusignan *Coups d'Œil et Coups de Plume* pp. 283–8
4 AHF to Aurelia Howells, Jan. 1878 (VDF)
5 See Robert M. Dawson *The Civil Service of Canada* chapter 2
6 AHF to Howells family, 1 Nov. 1878 (VDF)
7 Most of AF's drawings and paintings were sold privately or disappeared in the course of accident and time. Only a few examples of his portrait work are in the possession of his grandsons. There is a detailed account of his early career as an artist, however, in Lusignan *Coups d'Œil* pp. 297–303, which mentions several of his paintings and describes his Art Association success of 1883. Among relevant correspondence on AF's artistic efforts: AF to AHF, 26 May 1879 (VDF) mentions his portrait of Crémazie; AF to AHF, 13 April 1881 (VDF) mentions his portrait of Papineau; AF to AHF, 17 April 1881 (VDF) indicates that Achille took first prize for life drawing in a local competition; WDH to AHF, 27 March 1882 (Houghton) discusses Achille's ambition to study art in the United States; AHF to WDH, 7 March 1882 (VDF) mentions Achille's plans to study portrait painting in the US that summer; there are a series of brief notes and letters of introduction by WDH to help AF carry on his art studies in New York, dated 1882 (VDF);

AF to WCH, 3 Aug. 1882 (VDF) announces the death of Achille's father
and his temporary abandonment of art study; series of letters from AF to
AHF, autumn 1883 (VDF) describes his studies at the Art Students'
League, New York

8 AHF to Howells family, 20 Feb. 1881 (VDF)
9 AHF 'The Chances of War, and How One Was Missed' *Harper's New
   Monthly Magazine* LXIII (Sept. 1881) 608
10 AHF to family, 15 Aug. 1882; WDH to WCH, 31 Dec. 1882 (VDF)
11 Waite *Canada 1874–1896* p. 93
12 'Literary Earnings' in ms notebook of AHF (VDF)
13 AHF to WDH, 15 May 1881 (VDF)
14 WDH to Victoria Howells, 21 July 1882 *Life in Letters* I p. 314
15 AHF to LF, 8 June 1880 (Public Archives of Canada)
16 Edmond Fréchette to AHF, 30 June 1878 (VDF)
17 The mss of Edmond Fréchette's contributions to the *Youth's Companion* are
   in the Huntington Library
18 Victoria Howells to WDH, 26 Dec. 1876 (VDF)
19 AHF to WDH, 17 Oct. 1877 (VDF)
20 WDH *My Mark Twain* p. 71

NOTES TO CHAPTER 7

1 AHF to WCH, 5 Jan. 1884 (VDF)
2 AF to WCH, 29 Jan. 1884 (VDF)
3 For detailed discussions of the status of bilingual separate schools in Ontario, see C.B. Sissons *Church and State in Canadian Education* chapter 1;
   Franklin A. Walker *Catholic Education and Politics in Ontario* passim; Marilyn
   Barber 'The Ontario Bilingual Schools Issue: Sources of Conflict' in
   Minorities, Schools and Politics ed Craig Brown pp. 63–84
4 'Self-assertive Teachers' *The Ottawa Citizen* 19 Sept. 1888
5 'Trustee to Priest' *Citizen* 20 Oct. 1888
6 'Affaire des Ecoles séparées' *Le Canada* 25 oct.–18 nov. 1888
7 'Lettre d'un Membre du Bureau des Ecoles séparées' *Le Canada* 19 nov.
   1888
8 'The Archbishop and the Schools: an Open Letter from Trustee Fréchette'
   Ottawa Evening Journal 21 Dec. 1889
9 'Mr. Fréchette to Rev. Father Whelan' *Journal* 5 Sept. 1893
10 'Mr. Fréchette's Retort Courteous' *Journal* 7 Sept. 1893
11 'Les Frères de la Doctrine chrétienne: Assemblée considérable de leurs
   anciens élèves' *Le Canada* 26 mars 1895
12 'Nos Ecoles locales – finie la Comédie' *Le Temps* 27 mars 1895

NOTES TO CHAPTER 8

1 WDH to AHF, 29 Aug. 1883 (VDF). This letter also mentions Gilder's response. The reaction of the *Harper's* editor is in H.M. Alden to AHF 31 May 1883 (Huntington)
2 AHF to WDH, 18 Nov. 1886 (VDF)
3 WDH to AHF, 28 Nov. 1886 (VDF)
4 WDH to WCH, 6 Feb. 1887 (Huntington)
5 WDH to AHF, 12 Dec. 1897 (Huntington)
6 There is a voluminous correspondence relating to the children's books, between AHF and the American Baptist Publication Society, and between AHF and E.W. Thomson, all in the possession of VDF. Other relevant correspondence includes WDH to AHF, 3 June 1900 (Houghton), explaining the copyright problems involved in placing the books in the hands of some other American publisher, and George N. Morang to AHF, 27 Nov. 1900 (VDF)
7 WDH to AHF, 12 Oct. 1888 (Houghton)
8 AHF to Aurelia Howells, 12 Feb. 1891 (VDF)
9 AHF to Aurelia, 29 May 1892 (VDF)
10 Unidentified newspaper clipping (VDF)
11 AHF to Aurelia Howells, 6 Dec. 1897 (VDF)
12 William Brymner to AF, 5 March 1888 (VDF)
13 AF to AHF, 28 Nov. 1901 (VDF)
14 Le Moine *Maple Leaves* pp. 309–10
15 WDH to AHF, 12 Sept. 1895 (Huntington)

NOTES TO CHAPTER 9

1 WDH to Aurelia Howells, 3 July 1897 (VDF). The revised ms of *Reuben Dale* is in the possession of VDF
2 AF 'J'ai Cinquante Ans!' Supplément musical au *Passe-Temps* v no 113 (22 juillet 1899)
3 AHF to Aurelia Howells, 10 June 1891 (VDF)
4 'Une Protestation' *Le Temps* 8 juin 1897
5 LF to AHF, 18 April 1899 (VDF)
6 The activities of this association are briefly summarized in James B. Hedges *Building the Canadian West* pp. 164–5
7 'What a Woman Saw in the West' *Mail and Empire* 14 July 1906
8 Ibid. 7 July 1906
9 WDH to AHF, 29 June 1906 (Houghton)
10 H. Vanderhoof of the *Inter-Ocean* to AHF, 6 July 1906 (VDF)

11 WDH to AHF, 28 Sept. 1906 (Houghton)
12 'Editor's Easy Chair' *Harper's Monthly Magazine* cxiv (Jan. 1907) 320
13 Ibid. 318; *Their Wedding Journey* p. 219
14 *Life in Letters* ii p. 242
15 AF to AHF, 1 May 1908 (VDF)

NOTES TO CHAPTER 10

1 AF *Report on the Enquiry Requested by the Board of Internal Economy of the House of Commons* ... p. 7
2 H.M. Alden to AHF, 7 Nov. 1912 and 21 Jan. 1913 (VDF). The typescripts of the two stories are in the possession of VDF
3 AHF 'His First-Born' *McClure's* xxxix (Sept. 1912) 571
4 WDH to AHF, 17 Jan. 1913 (Houghton)
5 AHF to Paul Kester, 2 Sept. 1917 (Paul Kester Papers, New York Public Library)
6 Typescript, and printed greeting card, dated 'Lausanne, 31 déc., 1916' (VDF)
7 'Remembrances of Switzerland in Peace and War,' a paper read by AHF on 28 Nov. 1919, in 'de Normandie Hall,' Ottawa (ms, VDF); 'Chanson d'Automne,' and translation 'Autumn Song,' by 'E.W.T.,' unidentified newspaper clippings, one dated 25 Oct. 1920 (VDF)
8 VDF, oral communication
9 AHF to Howells Fréchette, 1 Oct. 1936 (VDF)

A Selected Bibliography

MANUSCRIPT COLLECTIONS

Fréchette Family Papers, in possession of Prof. Van Derck Fréchette
Howells Collection, Houghton Library, Harvard University
Howells-Fréchette Collection, Huntington Library, San Marino, Calif.
Howells Collection, Rutherford B. Hayes Library, Fremont, Ohio
Louis Fréchette Papers, Public Archives of Canada
Paul Kester Papers, New York Public Library
Whitelaw Reid Papers, Library of Congress
W.H. Smith Papers, Ohio Historical Society

ACHILLE FRÉCHETTE: PUBLISHED WORKS

'A la Mémoire de Madame E.H. St.-Denis, née Fréchette.' *Le Foyer domestique* I
  (1 juillet 1876) 306
'J'ai Cinquante Ans!' *Le Passe-Temps* V no. 113 (22 juillet 1899)
'Les Martyrs de la Foi au Canada.' *La Revue canadienne* V (sept. 1868)
  678–85
'L'Irlande: Romance.' *L'Opinion publique* II (19 oct. 1871) 504
'Quand on fait son droit.' *La Revue canadienne* VIII (mars 1871) 200–1
*Report on the Enquiry Requested by the Board of Internal Economy of the House of
  Commons of Canada to be Made in Belgium and Switzerland by Mr. Achille Fréchette,
  I.S.O.* [Ottawa: King's Printer 1910]
'Sit ei Terra levis.' *A la Mémoire de Alphonse Lusignan. Hommage de ses Amis et
  Confrères*. Montréal: Desaulniers et Leblanc 1892
'Souvenir d'Enfance.' *Le Souvenir* 1921 6

ANNIE HOWELLS FRÉCHETTE: PUBLISHED WORKS

'A Banner Divorce County.' *The Century* XXXVII (Feb. 1900) 636–40
'A Visit to a Country-House, and What Came of It.' *Harper's New Monthly Magazine* LV (Sept. 1877) 604–10
'A Widow in the Wilderness.' *Harper's New Monthly Magazine* C (Dec. 1899) 159–60
'Fireworks.' *The Galaxy* XIV (Sept. 1872) 398–401
'Frightened Eyes.' *Our Young Folks* IV (May 1868) 309–11
'His First-Born.' *McClure's* XXXIX (Sept. 1912) 562–72
'How Cassie Saved the Spoons.' *McClure's* I (Sept. 1893) 301–8. Reprinted in *Tales from McClure's: Adventure*. New York: Doubleday & McClure 1897.
'How That Cup Slipped.' *Harper's New Monthly Magazine* LIX (Sept. 1879) 589–94
'Isabel, Elsie, and I.' *New England Magazine* III (Oct. 1890) 249–55
'Le Coureur des Bois.' *Scribner's Monthly* [*The Century*] XII (May 1876) 108–17
'Life at Rideau Hall.' *Harper's New Monthly Magazine* LXIII (July 1881) 213–23
'Love Has a Conscience.' *The Ottawa Journal* 13 April 1895 17
'McDonald and Company, Builders.' *Harper's Bazar* XXI (20 Oct. 1888) 694–5
On Grandfather's Farm. Philadelphia: American Baptist Publication Society 1897
'Poor Little Bobby.' *The Youth's Companion* LI (30 May 1878) 171–2
Popular Sayings from Old Iberia. By 'Fieldat' [Eduardo Premio-Real] and 'Aitiache' [Annie T. Howells]. Quebec: Dawson & Co 1877
'Reuben Dale.' *The Galaxy* XX (Dec. 1875) 725–36; XXI (Jan. 1876) 56–74, (Feb. 1876) 208–18, (March 1876) 389–400, (April 1876) 505–12
'Summer Resorts on the St. Lawrence.' *Harper's New Monthly Magazine* LXIX (July 1884) 197–209
'The Chances of War, and How One Was Missed.' *Harper's New Monthly Magazine* LXIII (Sept. 1881) 603–8
The Farm's Little People. Philadelphia: American Baptist Publication Society 1897
'The Jones's Telephone.' *McClure's* I (Oct. 1893) 394–8. Reprinted in *Tales from McClure's: Humor*. New York: Doubleday & McClure 1897
'The Logic of Chance.' *New England Magazine* XX (Aug. 1899) 669–76
'William Dean Howells.' *Canadian Bookman* II (July 1920) 9–12

SECONDARY SOURCES

Brown, [Robert] Craig, ed. *Minorities, Schools and Politics*. Toronto: University of Toronto Press 1969

Brown, Robert Craig, and Ramsay Cook. *Canada 1896–1921: A Nation Transformed*. Toronto: McClelland & Stewart 1974

Cady, Edwin H. *The Road to Realism: The Early Years, 1837–1885, of William Dean Howells*. Syracuse: Syracuse University Press 1956

– *The Realist at War: The Mature Years, 1885–1920, of William Dean Howells*. Syracuse: Syracuse University Press 1958

Dassonville, Michel, ed. *Fréchette*. Montréal & Paris: Fides 1959

Dawson, Robert M. *The Civil Service of Canada*. London: Oxford University Press 1929

Eggleston, Wilfrid. *The Queen's Choice: A Story of Canada's Capital*. Ottawa: National Capital Commission 1961

Fréchette, Louis. *Mémoires intimes*. Ed. George A. Klinck. Montréal & Paris: Fides 1961

– *Poésies choisies* deuxième série. Montréal: Librairie Beauchemin 1908

Haig, Robert. *Ottawa: City of the Big Ears*. Ottawa: Haig & Haig 1969

Hedges, James B. *Building the Canadian West: The Land and Colonization Policies of the Canadian Pacific Railway*. New York: Macmillan 1939

Howells, William Dean. *A Boy's Town*. 1890; rpt. Westport, Conn.: Greenwood Press 1970

– *A Chance Acquaintance*. Boston: J.R. Osgood 1873

– 'Editor's Easy Chair' [on Ottawa] *Harper's Monthly Magazine* CXIV (Jan. 1907) 317–20

– *Life in Letters of William Dean Howells*. Ed. Mildred Howells. 2 vols. Garden City, N.Y.: Doubleday, Doran 1928

– *Literary Friends and Acquaintance*. New York & London: Harper & Brothers, 1901

– *My Literary Passions*. 1895; rpt. New York: Greenwood Press 1969

– *My Mark Twain*. New York & London: Harper & Brothers 1910

– 'Recent Literature [rev. of *Popular Sayings from Old Iberia*].' *Atlantic Monthly* XL (Sept. 1877) 377–8

– *Representative Selections*. Ed. Clara M. Kirk and Rudolf Kirk. New York: Hill & Wang 1961

– *The Vacation of the Kelwyns*. New York: Harper & Brothers 1920

– *Their Wedding Journey*. Boston: J.R. Osgood 1872

– *Years of My Youth*. New York & London: Harper & Brothers 1916

James, Henry. 'Quebec.' *Portraits of Places*. Boston: J.R. Osgood 1884

Klinck, George A. *Louis Fréchette, prosateur*. Lévis: Le Quotidien 1955

Le Moine, James. *Maple Leaves, 7th Series*. Quebec: Frank Carrel 1906

Lusignan, Alphonse. *Coups d'Œil et Coups de Plume*. Ottawa: Les Ateliers du 'Free Press' 1884

Mayer, Harold M. and Richard C. Wade. *Chicago: Growth of a Metropolis.* Chicago & London: University of Chicago Press 1969

Minton, Eric. *Ottawa: Reflections of the Past.* Toronto: Nelson, Foster and Scott 1974

Roseboom, Eugene H. *The Civil War Era: 1850–1873.* A History of the State of Ohio Vol. IV. Columbus: Ohio State Archaeological and Historical Society 1944

Serre, Lucien. *Louis Fréchette: Notes pour servir à la biographie du poète.* Montréal: Les Frères de Ecoles chrétiennes 1928

Sissons, C.B. *Church and State in Canadian Education.* Toronto: Ryerson 1959

Thoreau, Henry D. *A Yankee in Canada.* Montreal: Harvest House 1961

Wade, Mason. *The French-Canadian Outlook.* 1946; rpt. Toronto: McClelland & Stewart 1964

Waite, Peter B. *Canada 1874–1896: Arduous Destiny.* Toronto: McClelland & Stewart 1971

Walker, Franklin A. *Catholic Education and Politics in Ontario.* Toronto: Thomas Nelson & Sons 1964

Weir, George M. *The Separate School Question in Canada.* Toronto: Ryerson Press 1934

Weisenburger, Francis P. *The Passing of the Frontier: 1825–1850.* A History of the State of Ohio Vol. III. Columbus: Ohio State Archaeological and Historical Society 1941

Index

This book
was designed by
ANTJE LINGNER
and was printed by
University of
Toronto
Press